THE FINANCIAL RELAY

NAVIGATING WEALTH ACROSS GENERATIONS

48 NARRATIVES AND 312 APPROACHES TO HELP THE
MODERN INDIAN FAMILY HONOR THE PAST, EMBRACE THE PRESENT,
AND SECURE THEIR FINANCIAL FUTURE

GARVIT CHAHARIA

INDIA · SINGAPORE · MALAYSIA

ISBN
Paperback 979-8-89699-511-1
Hardcase 979-8-89777-288-9

CONTENTS

About the Author 7

Prologue 9

RUN

1. The Price of Ambition 17

2. The Joy of Planning 21

3. Earnings Are Not Everything 25

4. Fix the Leak .29

5. Invisible Wealth 35

6. Shining Trap .41

7. Legacy in Limbo 47

8. The Price of Plenty 53

9. Needs to Dream 57

10. Wisdom of Time 61

11. True Investment Value 65

12. Locked Wealth 71

13. Taming Fear .75

14. Work Smarter, Not Harder 81

15. Shifting Priorities 85

16. Growth on Autopilot 91

17. Goal First, Strategy Next 95

18. Shortcuts and Setbacks 99

19. The Business Mindset 103

20. Past Is Not Proof 109

21. Ride the Risk 113

22. Power of Patience 119

23. Blooming Amidst Storms 125

24. No Pit-stops 129

25. The Power of Letting Go 135

26. Rise or Die 139

27. Exit Before It is Too Late 143

28. The Right Mix 147

29. Safety First 153

30. The Myth of All-in-one 159

31. Why White Wins 165

32. The Emotional Reward 169

33. Choose Your Poison 173

34. More is Less 177

35. Free is a Gimmick 181

36. Risky Reels 185

37. The DIY Effect 189

38. The Blame Game 195

REAP

39. Move On 201

40. Shades of Money 205

41. Betting on Tomorrow. 209

REST

42. Living with Freedom 215

43. Money Works for You 221

44. The Net Worth Mirage 225

45. The Exit Strategy. .229

46. Perfect on Paper. 235

47. Untold Burdens 241

48. When Wisdom Fails. 245

Epilogue 249

ABOUT THE AUTHOR

Garvit Chaharia is a Certified Financial Planner with a passion for simplifying the often-complex world of personal finance. Over the years he has found immense satisfaction in helping entrepreneurs and professionals navigate their financial journeys with clarity and confidence. His approach blends modern technology with deep interpersonal skills to provide tailored solutions that truly serve his clients' needs.

Garvit's career began with the family-owned saree business, but when the venture collapsed, he realised the transformative power of resilience and reinvention. Transitioning to financial advisory was a deliberate choice, as it is a field that requires minimal resources to start but demands exceptional dedication and consistency. He began his financial career in 2007 and incorporated *DV Mint* a firm committed to helping individuals and families achieve financial security and prosperity.

Beyond finance, Garvit is passionate about fitness and running. He firmly believes that wealth has little value without good health, and makes it a point to incorporate discipline and balance into every aspect of his life. His first book, *The FinVisor's Mojo*, guides financial advisors on mastering the emotional intelligence necessary to connect with clients and build long-lasting, valuable relationships.

Through *The Financial Relay,* Garvit wants to share his insights and experiences to help others achieve financial success and live more fulfilling lives.

PROLOGUE

Life is a relay race that stretches across generations. The baton you are holding isn't just any stick; it's the embodiment of your ancestors' financial struggles, triumphs, and the foundation they built. This baton represents not just a legacy but the responsibilities and opportunities that come with it. Your challenge is to not drop the baton you receive, run your leg of the race with purpose and ensure the baton you pass on is even stronger and more secure for the next generation. If at any point in the race, you end up dropping the baton, it will break your momentum, and you will take longer to finish the race or end up losing it all altogether.

The Financial Relay: A Journey of Legacy and Responsibility

In this relay race, there are three crucial legs: taking responsibility for the baton, running with it to achieve your financial goals, and finally, passing it on with care and preparation. This book is divided into three stages to reflect this journey, guiding you through each phase with practical advice and actionable insights.

RUN

Running Your Leg of the Race

With the baton in hand, this phase typically marks a period of focused effort and momentum. It's a time to harness the stability and resources you've been given, using them to build a secure and prosperous present. People often find themselves using the strength of this foundation to move forward, whether that's through advancing their careers, making thoughtful investments, or planning for future financial needs.

At this stage, managing finances wisely becomes a key priority. Many focus on setting and saving for long-term goals, carefully balancing present needs with future ambitions. The baton, symbolic of what's been passed down or earned, often serves as a springboard to help individuals navigate their financial decisions, whether it's managing risk, exploring new opportunities, or preparing for inevitable expenses.

This period is also about making strategic choices that support long-term success. It's not just about achieving personal milestones but also laying the groundwork for the future. Planning for retirement, mitigating risks, and staying adaptable to changing circumstances are common considerations during this phase, and how effectively these challenges are managed can shape the overall financial journey.

REAP

Taking Responsibility for the Baton

This leg of the race often begins when you inherit the baton from your ancestors. This phase is typically about more than just receiving financial assets; it involves understanding the emotional significance and the weight of the legacy passed down. While your ancestors may have laid the foundation, the responsibility to nurture and grow it usually falls on the next generation.

At this stage, most people start by assessing what they have inherited—whether it's savings, investments, or even debts. It's common to reflect on the financial habits of those who came before, taking note of both their successes and the challenges they faced. By learning from their experiences, many aim to avoid repeating past mistakes while continuing to build on the achievements left behind.

Inheriting typically happens once in a lifetime, and this moment can carry a sense of urgency. There is often a focus on handling it carefully, recognising that mistakes made during this phase can be difficult to correct. It's a delicate balance of honouring the past while ensuring a stable future.

REST

Passing the Baton Safely

In the final leg of the race, the focus shifts to passing the baton to the next generation. This stage is pivotal, as the way assets and responsibilities are handed over can shape the future financial path of your family.

Rather than just transferring wealth, this phase often involves preparing the next generation with the knowledge and tools to navigate their own financial journeys. It's about instilling a sense of financial responsibility, encouraging thoughtful investing, and fostering an understanding of the importance of long-term planning.

The aim is typically to make this transition as seamless as possible, allowing the next generation to confidently take the lead. Ideally, the baton becomes a source of support and empowerment, helping them build on the foundation already in place.

As this process unfolds, many also find themselves gradually stepping back, creating space for personal fulfilment, hobbies, and a slower pace of life. It's a time to reflect, ensuring that by the end of the journey, there are no lingering regrets.

The financial relay race is more than just a metaphor; it's a reflection of how we handle our financial responsibilities across generations. Many believe that our only responsibility is to earn, but we also have two other critical responsibilities. It's about **Run. Reap. Rest.**

It's about honouring the past, embracing the present, and securing the future. Each leg of the race requires dedication, strategy, and careful planning.

By taking responsibility for the baton, running with purpose, and passing it on with care, you ensure that your financial legacy is not only preserved but also enhanced. This journey is a testament to the power of mindful financial management and the importance of securing a prosperous future for those who will follow.

If we knowingly or unknowingly drop the baton at any stage of the race, it can lead to delays and disappointments. Similarly, poor financial decisions can result in setbacks that prevent us from reaching our goals on time. Setting realistic expectations and understanding that everyone's objectives differ—whether you want to win the race or just enjoy it—ensures that the journey remains enjoyable, easy, and comfortable. It has to ultimately be your OWN goal. Only then will you be motivated to achieve it.

There is an abundance of financial help books available in the market. This book is designed for the Indian mindset, offering insights tailored to diverse financial scenarios and challenges, including Indian needs, desires, family dynamics, and emotional and social aspects. Western financial principles may not always be suitable for Indian society.

Everyone is pursuing financial knowledge, but knowledge alone is not enough; mindset and behaviour go hand in hand. This book will help you build the right mindset. Knowledge without implementation is futile. Even a single change in mindset can make a significant difference in your life. Our vision is to help people attain financial independence where money becomes a source of happiness, not stress.

RUN

The "Run" phase is the longest and most demanding period of your financial journey. It begins when you start earning your own money, managing it to meet both personal goals and family needs and taking on the responsibilities that come with financial independence.

This phase is characterised by growth, discipline, and resilience. It's also the most aggressive phase of life, where we often face immense peer pressure and the desire to stay ahead. This drive can lead to running blindly, losing sight of our true goals. We sometimes forget why we started running in the first place or why we are earning money at all.

If we accumulate wealth but fail to use our time or money to enrich our lives, we've lost focus. During the "Run" phase, we must balance our goals, health, and time, alongside family and social life.

The longer this phase lasts, the greater the opportunity for mistakes. It's a period of learning, growth, and sometimes missteps, which is why it's so important to remain mindful. The "Run" phase doesn't just start when you begin earning—it starts the day you're born, with your parents preparing you for this journey. Earning money, gaining respect, taking on responsibilities, and discovering the purpose of your life all take shape in this foundational phase.

Chapter – 01

THE PRICE OF AMBITION

In the bustling heart of Pune, lived Mohit. His life revolved around his small, modest restaurant, 'Mohit's Delight', which he and his wife Naina had opened with their precious savings.

Family meant everything to Mohit and he wanted to give them every luxury and comfort imaginable. Driven by passion and determination, he poured everything he had into the restaurant, putting in long hours, blood, sweat, and tears.

The early days were a struggle. Mohit served as chef, waiter, accountant—any role the restaurant required him to play. Slowly but surely, his dedication began to pay off. The aroma of his signature dishes wafted through the streets, and word of mouth turned his modest establishment into a neighbourhood gem. Over time, the restaurant evolved into a successful family establishment.

With each passing day, Mohit's business grew, as did his profits. 'Mohit's Delight' wasn't just a restaurant; it was a place to nurture community, share stories and laughter, and celebrate birthdays and anniversaries.

The restaurant's success was a testament to Mohit's relentless determination and his commitment to quality.

As the years went by, the profits rolled in, and Mohit's net worth grew. He could now afford to give his family the life he had always wanted. He had always promised to take them on an international vacation but decided that it wasn't time yet. He wanted to expand his business instead. After making provisions for daily expenses, he invested all the remaining profits back into the restaurant and decided to open a second outlet. His vision was to open a chain of restaurants and build a legacy for his children to carry on in the future.

Will a second restaurant bring his family true happiness? More money might come from a chain, but will he truly enjoy it?

Points to Ponder:

1. Psychologist Abraham Maslow's Hierarchy of Needs reminds us that true satisfaction comes in stages. Only once you fulfil your basic, material needs can you move on to things like love and spirituality. Therefore, there was nothing wrong with Mohit's ambition and wanting to build a business.

2. Money can buy you happiness. But happiness doesn't come from money just lying in the bank—it's the experiences and memories we build using money that bring us joy. And that is where Mohit fumbled.

3. Mohit should have also remembered to financially plan for fun and quality time with his family. He invested everything he earned to build a big and

profitable business but forgot to save for what's actually important—life experiences, the future of his children & financial security. Now, at the age of 60, Mohit has multiple successful restaurants all over the city but he is not happy. He has only ever earned money but never spent it.

"Money earned isn't joy; money spent is."

Chapter – 02

THE JOY OF PLANNING

Meera and Krish, along with their friends Gauri and Om, were eagerly planning a long-awaited vacation to Bali. Two months before the trip, they gathered at Meera and Krish's home to finalise the details. The atmosphere was buzzing with excitement as they discussed flight options, accommodations, and activities.

After hours of research, they booked flight tickets and a cosy villa in the heart of Bali. Gauri, always the meticulous planner, insisted they pre-book ferry tickets to explore the nearby islands at their own pace. They even came up with a daily food budget to ensure they had enough money left for other experiences like shopping and adventure sports. Although Meera and Krish preferred spontaneity, they agreed, wanting to make the most of their time in Bali.

As they delved into planning their itinerary, Gauri and Om suggested booking tickets in advance for some of the famous monuments to avoid long queues. Meera and Krish, envisioning a more flexible vacation, initially hesitated. After a friendly debate, they compromised and agreed to pre-book tickets for two key monuments. They then decided to look for fun, unique activities. They were thrilled to see videos of tourists scuba diving. However, after checking the price, which went over their budget, they decided to go snorkelling instead of compromising on the overall quality of their vacation.

A week before the departure date, Om reminded everyone to apply for a Forex card. Gauri and Om were quick to embrace this convenient option, but Krish was adamant about exchanging currency upon arrival, convinced he could get a better exchange rate.

The day of the trip arrived, and the excitement peaked. They reached the airport with their bags, passports, and Meera's wallet, which contained some emergency cash. However, Krish realised he had forgotten his wallet, which held the majority of the funds earmarked for the trip.

Panic set in momentarily, but Meera reassured him, and they decided to contact the bank upon reaching Bali to figure out a solution. Upon landing, Krish quickly reached out to his bank, only to receive a notification about the system being down for development and maintenance.

Luckily, most of their expenses, including accommodation and pre-booked activities, had already been paid for. Om and Gauri's Forex card became a lifeline for the group, covering immediate expenses like meals and local transport. While the rest of the group was exploring Bali, Krish could not enjoy the trip. His money situation was constantly stressing him out. Finally, on the third day, the bank's system was back up, and Krish could access his money. Relieved and grateful, Krish reimbursed Om and Gauri immediately. Now that they had some funds left, they finally decided to stop holding back and go shopping. Meanwhile, Meera and Krish's suggestion of not pre-booking all the activities gave them the time and opportunity to explore Bali in a leisurely manner and visit niche spots suggested by the locals, making the rest of the trip a happy memory.

Which financial plan would you follow? Who managed their priorities better and avoided issues?

Points to Ponder:

4. Just as we plan our vacations and our lives, we also need to plan our financial journey wisely and ensure our money is both safe and accessible. Budgeting is like a roadmap that helps us make smart choices about saving and spending. By setting a daily budget for food, the two couples ensured they had enough money to enjoy their trip. When you know how much you have, you can then easily gauge what your limits are.

5. Prioritising is another important part of the plan. We all have needs and wants, but we can't do everything at once. The group made smart choices in various instances to make their vacation better. They began by spending on the basics—travel, stay and food. Only after they had sorted out the necessities, did they start planning their experiences and after all that did they decide to spend it on shopping and partying. Similarly, in life, we need to prioritise our needs over our wants.

6. When we earn, we usually budget for our basic needs first, then move on to our static financial goals which include expenses like raising children, their education, their wedding, buying a house, and planning our retirement. Only once all of this is done are we supposed to enjoy the surplus. That surplus can be used guilt-free on all our wants and desires.

7. However, the goal of planning is not to stress us out; it's to help us enjoy life and the money we make. It is also important to remember that one need not save everywhere; it is okay to spend. Om and Gauri picked the safe and secure Forex card over getting a slightly better exchange rate. This helped a lot when Krish forgot his wallet, making sure they had money and could enjoy Bali without problems. Having the funds before starting the vacation makes you stress-free, just like having funds at the beginning of a financial goal.

8. When a small travel plan of a few days requires so much planning. A tiny monetary hiccup made Krish and Meera's experience so stressful. Imagine how stressful it can be if you don't have money at the time you need it for actual emergencies. What gets measured gets done . The challenge only arises when you don't plan for and are unable to achieve something that you have aspired to.

"Life is a holiday when planned well."

Chapter – 03

EARNINGS ARE NOT EVERYTHING

In the 1980s, Mighty T was a prodigy in heavyweight boxing. With a ferocious style and an undeniable charisma, he rose to become the youngest heavyweight champion of the world at the age of 20. With a string of quick and devastating victories, Mighty T's fame transcended the sport, making him a global icon.

As T's career skyrocketed, so did his spending habits. Mansions adorned with extravagant furnishings, a fleet of luxury cars, and a collection of exotic pets became hallmarks of the young champion's lifestyle. Lavish parties, designer clothing, and an insatiable desire for excess characterised his daily existence. It seemed as though his wealth would never run dry, and he lived under an illusion of eternal prosperity.

The peril of having unlimited aspirations with finite resources became increasingly apparent as T's spending outpaced his income. Despite earning millions from his highly publicised boxing matches, Tyson found himself ensnared in a web of debt.

T's troubles outside the ring further pushed him towards his financial downfall. Legal battles, including a highly publicised divorce, tarnished his reputation and further drained his finances. The once-invincible champion found himself on the ropes, both professionally and personally. The excessive lifestyle that once appeared sustainable now was on the verge of collapsing.

Despite earning an estimated $300 million throughout his career, Mighty T's financial empire crumbled under the weight of his extravagant lifestyle and mounting legal fees.

By 2003, the man who had once commanded hundreds of millions of dollars in the boxing ring was filing for bankruptcy.

In the years that followed, he faced the consequences of his financial mismanagement. Having learned his lesson, T embarked on a journey of self-discovery, acknowledging his mistakes, and attempting to rebuild his life both inside and outside the ring.

Did you ever think it was possible to be in debt despite earning as much as Mighty T? Was it because his dreams outpaced his income?

Points to Ponder:

9. Right from birth, we're conditioned to be successful. Scoring high marks, earning good money, and taking care of what we value—most of us are taught these lessons young. Here's the tricky part: considering that we start earning around 25 and retire around 60, we only earn for approximately 35 years of our life and only spend for the rest of it. It is our responsibility to

be able to sustain the money we have made for the rest of our years. It's like a seesaw, with our aspirations on one end and our resources on the other. Now, as a family breadwinner, juggling limited resources with big dreams and providing for other people, can be challenging.

10. Setting goals is very important to stay on track. But the actual challenge lies in when you have wrong aspirations or above-average expectations that do not match with your lifestyle.

11. While Mighty T had single-handedly earned more money than most could ever dream of, he soon lost it all owing to the lack of sound financial planning. All the years of hard work he put in from a young age to bring himself out of the poverty he was born in, went down the drain over a couple of years. At the end of the day, it is not about how much you earn, but how much you spend. It's time to nurture the seed of limited resources and cultivate a mindset that balances our big dreams with practical choices.

"Dream big but spend within your means."

FIX THE LEAK

In the serene town of Indrapur, set against the backdrop of mystical mountains and meandering rivers, there resided a man named Rajji. Indrapur was renowned for its unpredictable winters, where snowfall could turn the town into a winter wonderland and make it nearly impossible to venture outdoors. Determined to prepare for the approaching winter, Rajji devised a plan during the warmth of summer.

Every day, as the sun set painted the sky in hues of orange and pink, Rajji came back home from work and diligently poured a large glass of rice into a large crock pot. He intended to amass a sufficient supply to endure the biting cold when winter arrived. The crock pot, a sturdy vessel, stood against the kitchen wall, tucked away in a corner.

However, to Rajji's dismay, he soon noticed that the pot was mysteriously filling up only halfway, no matter how much rice he poured into it. Puzzled, he persisted, thinking perhaps it was a trick of the light. Yet, each day, the level of rice remained stubbornly fixed.

On the fourth day, frustration crept into Rajji's mind, and he was compelled to investigate the cause of the curious phenomenon. He decided to inspect the crock pot closely. To his surprise, when he turned it around, a small hole revealed itself at the back. A leak, unnoticed until then, was the culprit behind the diminishing rice level.

Rajji pulled out the crock pot from its corner and discovered a mound of rice that had seeped out. He looked at the mound of rice in despair as it had now been infested. The realisation struck him like a cold gust of wind. The leak had been robbing him of his carefully stored provisions.

What should Rajji fix first to stop wasting food? How can controlling what goes out help him achieve this?

Points to Ponder:

12. Even though Rajji was working hard to save up for the winter, it was all in vain. Unless Rajji fixed the hole in his crockpot first, there was no point in him trying to save the rice he worked so hard for, it was going to go to waste anyway. Similarly, if you don't fix the hole in your wallet, you might not end up with much in your bank account. However hard you work to earn money, it's all going to leak out through that hole called overspending.

13. Overspending delays our investments messes up our EMI payments and puts a wrench in our financial goals. We spend for our enjoyment and then end up feeling guilty afterwards. But if we have already

paid off our EMI instalments and invested towards our goal, there's no reason for us to feel guilty while spending. Usually, overspending happens because calculating budgets is a hassle, and we lack discipline and self-control. How can we fix this?

14. Adults can be as simplistic in their thinking when it comes to complex calculations. People often spend money from the same account where they get their income. This means they look at all the money in their bank account as their spending limit. This makes it hard for them to know when to stop.

15. But here's an idea: have two different bank accounts. One is for your income (where your salary, investment money and money towards EMI go), and the other is for your expenses (your monthly spending budget). You need to transfer money from your income account into your expenses account as per your spending budget every month. And so, by separating your accounts, you make sure that there is a limit to the amount of spending money in front of you. You can even make the spending account a joint account with someone you trust. This way, you're answerable to someone for your spending. Knowing that someone else can also see how much and what you are spending will stop you from binge shopping.

16. Disable UPI transactions and don't carry the debit card on you for the income account. This makes it harder to spend money that is above your budget by adding an additional step. You will have to manually

transfer extra money from your income account into your expenses account. This additional step will make you think twice before you transfer that additional money and spend it.

17. Planning is crucial. Time your investments and EMI for the same week you get your salary. This regularises your investments and EMI and will ensure that you take care of important things first. This helps you avoid problems later in the month and gives you a clear idea of how much money you have for your everyday expenses. By making all the payments and investments first you will realise how much money you can actually transfer into your expenditure account and spend only that amount every month.

18. Using a credit card isn't always a bad thing, but it can lead to overspending. If you have a big purchase in mind that you can afford, you can always decide to put it on your credit card to pay in instalments. This way, you are ensuring your liquidity while maintaining control over your spending. One powerful way to curb overspending is by setting a lower limit on your credit card, even if you can afford a higher one. When faced with a big purchase, you'll need to manually increase your limit, creating an extra step in the process. Just like with our income account, this also gives you a chance to pause and reconsider whether that purchase is really necessary.

19. To stop overspending, you need to change your thinking and take practical steps. By following these

simple strategies, you can control your money better, avoid unnecessary spending, and set yourself up for a more secure financial future.

"Save first, spend smart."

Chapter – 05

INVISIBLE WEALTH

In a vast jungle, where the sun filtered through dense foliage, lived a magnificent herd of elephants. Among them was Bhima, a mighty elephant with grand, shimmering tusks that made him the undisputed leader. The animals revered him, believing his tusks symbolised his strength. In contrast, Raghu, another elephant with no visible tusks, was often overlooked and underestimated.

One scorching summer, a fierce drought gripped the jungle, drying rivers and withering vegetation. Amid this turmoil, a cunning tiger named Sheru saw an opportunity. Hungry and thirsty, he decided to challenge the elephants, aiming to hunt the strongest among them.

Sheru ambushed the herd, leaping towards Bhima. A fierce battle ensued, with Bhima swinging his mighty tusks. But Sheru was swift, dodging the heavy blows. As Bhima grew weary, his tusks seemed more a burden than a boon. Seizing the moment, Sheru lunged for a final attack.

Suddenly, Raghu charged forward. Without cumbersome tusks to hinder him, he manoeuvred with surprising speed and strength. He rammed into Sheru, knocking the tiger off balance. Raghu's true strength lay hidden. Beneath his lip were small yet formidable inner teeth. Unlike the others, he maintained his strength and energy.

Raghu's attack was relentless. He used his inner teeth to grab and twist, breaking Sheru's hold and throwing him aside. The tiger, realising his mistake, slunk away, defeated and humiliated.

The jungle fell silent as the herd gathered around Raghu; their eyes wide with awe. The quiet hum of the jungle resumed, leaving the inhabitants to ponder the day's events.

"Did Bhima's tusks reflect true worth in adversity? How do your assets hold up under pressure?"

Points to Ponder:

20. Your net worth can be classified into types, Fixed net worth and Liquid Net Worth. Fixed net worth encompasses assets that are not easily converted into cash. Fixed net worth includes assets like real estate, investments in personal businesses, used assets such as jewellery, the home you live in, cars, etc. These assets are crucial for capital appreciation, generate regular income and provide self-satisfaction, but they lack flexibility.

21. Fixed net worth is also known as 'social net worth'. Social net worth is akin to an elephant's tusks, showcasing our wealth and status in society. People generally take on loans to enhance their social net

worth, expand their business, purchasing larger homes, luxury cars, and other status symbols.

22. A common issue with social net worth is the emotional and societal value attached to these assets. We often equate our social status and personal worth with our property holdings, which can prevent us from making rational financial decisions. Even in times of financial need, the fear of losing face or respect in society may deter us from selling them. It hurts our emotions when we have to exit these assets, that is why fixed net worth is also known as emotional net worth.

23. It is also important to remember that used assets should not be considered a part of your net worth, they are possessions. The home that you live in, your car, jewellery—are necessities and personal purchases that you are more than allowed to make. But it's important to differentiate between personal necessities and financial investments while considering your finances. In most cases, you cannot and will not readily sell these in times of need.

24. When we are biased towards fixed net worth and ignore liquid net worth, we become financially handicapped because we can only spend our liquid net worth. This 'unusable net worth' limits our ability to address our financial needs, leading to financial instability. Relying solely on fixed assets without sufficient liquid assets can make it difficult to navigate unexpected expenses and opportunities.

25. Your liquid net worth is your liquid assets minus your liabilities. Liquid assets include ones that can be easily converted into cash. These assets provide the liquidity necessary for financial needs and offer a flexible cushion for unforeseen circumstances. Key components of liquid assets include cash and bank accounts, paper investments such as stocks, bonds, mutual funds, PPFs, etc., as well as precious metals like gold and silver bars and coins. These can be liquidated relatively quickly, although their value may fluctuate. Your liabilities on the other hand are any kind of personal and professional/business loans. The difference between these two is your actual liquid net worth.

26. While liquid net worth offers freedom and flexibility, it also comes with its disadvantages. Unlike fixed assets, liquid assets do not overtly display your social status, leading to a perception of lesser wealth. Moreover, liquidity can lead to increased spending, as the readily available money can be tempting to use. Despite these drawbacks, liquid net worth provides the power to live your life the way you want, with the ability to spend as needed.

27. The ideal scenario is to maintain a healthy balance between liquid and fixed assets. This balance allows us to have enough liquidity for our lifetime needs without sacrificing long-term wealth building through fixed assets. The recommended ratio is for fixed assets to make up no more than 70% of your

net worth, with liquid assets constituting at least 30%. This is a guiding rule that can vary based on your personal circumstances.

28. If not managed correctly, an imbalance in net worth can lead to debt and financial distress. Debts are paid in liquid assets and if you have to sell off your fixed assets in order to pay them, then the scenario is called bankruptcy. It's sad to see that most people in India have a negative liquid net worth, with large fixed assets financed by significant loans.

29. People often believe that liquid net worth does not build wealth. However, if you look at the historical data, liquid assets like equity have offered better returns over fixed assets like real estate and gold, along with the additional advantage of liquidity.

30. Bhima's tusks were impressive, but imagine if he had strong teeth like Raghu instead. He would not have crumbled when faced with sudden danger. Your social net worth may be impressive, but you need to have enough cash to spend throughout your lifetime and be able to settle debts and liabilities without having to sell your prized assets. What would make you happier — 3 crores in hand to spend and 7 crores in fixed assets or 7 crores to spend and 3 crores in fixed assets? If we manage to switch the ratio to favour more liquid assets, we can achieve financial happiness and stability.

"Net worth matters but liquidity rules."

Chapter – 06

SHINING TRAP

In the 1990s, Ramesh married Asha in a grand ceremony steeped in tradition. Asha was fond of jewellery, which is why as part of the rituals, her parents gifted her a substantial amount of gold jewellery, spending a considerable sum. Every time Asha's parents or in-laws gave her any gift money, be it for Diwali or a special occasion, she bought jewellery with it. In her mind, this was a smart decision because she could wear the jewellery and it acted as an investment. Asha often spoke with pride about how the jewellery would safeguard their future. Over the years, as the price of gold steadily rose, her confidence only grew.

Two decades later, Ramesh's business hit a rough patch, plunging him into a financial crisis. Desperate for funds to save his livelihood, he and Asha reluctantly considered selling the gold jewellery. The thought of parting with these precious pieces was heart-wrenching, as they symbolised their marriage, family heritage, and years of tradition.

They finally decided that they could not outright sell the jewellery and decided to pawn it instead. They were going to approach their regular jeweller, who was also a friend, but the shame of having to sell their jewellery prevented them from doing so. With a heavy heart, Ramesh visited the bank instead to pledge it, hoping the appreciated gold prices would fetch a substantial amount. However, they were in for a rude shock. Though the price of gold had indeed risen, the value of the jewellery was not as high as they had expected. The resale value reflected was a lot lower.

The realisation was a bitter pill to swallow. They had hoped that the jewellery would be their financial safety net, but the harsh truth was that the investment, despite its sentimental worth, did not yield the financial relief they needed. The value, both monetary and emotional, was not what they had once believed it to be.

Was gold jewellery an investment or a sentimental possession? If gold is a safe investment, why did Asha's wedding jewellery lose its value?

Points to Ponder:

31. As humans, we like to own things. It gives us a sense of stability. This is why so many of us, including Asha, feel safe buying assets that we can own, like gold. It is because the physicality of it gives us a sense of ownership.

32. The reason Ramesh and Asha's gold did not yield them the return they had expected was because it was gold jewellery and not gold bars or coins. When investing in gold jewellery there are several factors

to consider. Firstly, the purity of the gold might not be as much as what you paid for. Secondly, quantity matters; your gold jewellery isn't entirely made up of gold. When selling gold jewellery, you will only be paid for the weight of gold in it, and so even a small difference in weight can significantly affect the value. Additionally, with jewellery, there are making charges that can inflate the cost but do not contribute to its resale value.

33. Another thing we don't consider when buying gold jewellery as an investment is that it often carries sentimental value. It is passed down through generations, given as gifts, and worn on special occasions. This emotional attachment can sometimes overshadow the financial aspects of gold ownership.

34. Just like Ramesh and Asha felt uncomfortable selling their jewellery in times of need and decided to pledge it for a loan, most people will have a hard time parting with their jewellery. This decision will only build up more stress, because not only is Ramesh now worried about his business, but also about repaying the loan to get Asha's jewellery back. This is why gold jewellery should not be considered as an investment but as a possession. If you are looking to invest in physical gold, then buy gold bars and coins instead.

35. There is a belief that gold has given us high returns. This is because its value has risen at par with SENSEX, over the past fifteen to twenty years. But what we fail to consider is that when we invest in

markets, we don't invest only in SENSEX. We often invest in an aggressive and diversified portfolio, giving us much higher returns than SENSEX. While gold may preserve wealth, especially in times of economic distress, it does not multiply it in the way that a diversified stock portfolio can.

36. However, in terms of financial planning, gold has long held a revered position as a hedge against risk. Allocating 10-15% of your portfolio to gold can provide a buffer against these risks.

37. All our assets—stocks, bonds, mutual funds, real estate, bank accounts—are controlled by the government. In times of personal financial distress, the government can block our bank accounts and demat accounts if they wish to. Holding on to physical gold has safety challenges, but it is also in your control. Unlike stocks or bonds, which are essentially pieces of paper or digital entities, gold is tangible. You can hold it, store it, and have complete control over it. This physicality adds a level of security and can help you out in tough times.

38. In distressed economic scenarios, such as war or severe economic crises, gold often shines as a stable store of value. Unlike paper assets, like stocks or bonds, which can become worthless in extreme situations, gold maintains its value across borders and throughout history. This characteristic makes gold an essential part of a well-rounded financial

strategy, particularly for those concerned about potential economic upheavals.

39. Gold is also a global standard; it holds value universally, which is particularly reassuring in an interconnected world where currencies and economies can fluctuate widely. No matter where you are, gold is recognised and valued. This gives it a unique advantage as a tangible asset that transcends borders and political instability. While it may not offer the same growth potential as other investments, its ability to preserve value across borders and generations makes it an essential part of any diversified financial plan.

"Used assets don't add to your net worth"

Chapter – 07

LEGACY IN LIMBO

Once, a man paid an exorbitant sum for a goose that laid golden eggs. Convinced it was a smart investment; he believed the goose would secure his future and provide for his children and grandchildren. At first, the golden eggs came frequently, and the family prospered. They dreamed of wealth that would last for generations.

However, what the man didn't account for was the goose's life span and irregularity. Some days, the goose didn't lay any eggs at all. Worse, the care it required to keep laying golden eggs—special feed, a warm environment, and costly veterinary visits—began to add up.

The man's sons, having grown up in the shadow of the magical goose, never bothered to learn any trade or skill. They merely tended to the goose; confident it would continue to provide for them indefinitely.

But when the goose finally became too sick to produce eggs, its treatment, medicines and nutrition supplements, all began to pile up into significant costs. The man decided to sell the goose as he could no longer afford to take care of it, but he was unable to find a buyer. The goose eventually died, and the family was left stranded. The golden eggs had run out, and they had no means of income. Their dependence on the goose had left them unprepared for its eventual demise. With no other skills or means to support themselves, they faced an uncertain future, all their hopes dashed by the loss of the one thing they had relied on for years.

What they thought was security had become a trap, leaving them without direction when the source of their wealth was gone.

Can you rely on a goose to lay golden eggs forever? What happens when a legacy turns into a burden?

Points to Ponder:

40. Too many people think of real estate like a goose that lays golden eggs. It seems lucrative because they think they will get regular rental income. They think it can become a steady source of cash flow, but in actuality, there are many factors that they don't consider.

41. Like the man assumed that the goose would give him a golden egg daily without fail, when evaluating potential income, people often assume that all the property will be rented out all year round. However, this may not always be the case. You need to evaluate your occupancy ratio and occupancy tenure. Occupancy ratio is the percentage of your property that's occupied at any given point. Occupancy tenure is the length of time your property is consistently rented. Tenant turnover, seasonal demand, or

unexpected vacancies can all reduce the returns you expect.

42. Even if we earn lower rent than expected, we are still satisfied because we assume that the value of our property is increasing with time. However, appreciating property value is often a matter of perception. Older buildings tend to lose their usability and desirability over time, making it more difficult to attract tenants. This may be lower than expected, leaving you with a property that may be worth less than its potential.

43. Real estate can have impressive notional value on paper, but its real value is only determined by whether or not you can sell it at that price. In a soft market, you might struggle to sell your property at the desired price. What's more, larger or older properties tend to have limited buyers, which makes selling even more challenging.

44. A big reason as to why we buy real estate is because real estate is considered an asset for generations, and it will be useful for our children. But on the contrary, it might hinder their growth. They might become heavily reliant on them, leaving them unmotivated to excel on their own.

45. Another consideration is that if you invest heavily in properties in a city, you may inadvertently tie your children to that area. For example, owning multiple properties in a small town can restrict your

children's ability to relocate for better opportunities, particularly if the properties are difficult to sell. The asset that once seemed like a generational investment can quickly become a generational burden. Property disputes and emotional attachment may prevent family members from selling. Even if one person wants to sell their share, family involvement from others might hinder the sale. Returning to the property for its sale can also be a logistical challenge, especially if family members live far away and lack the time to manage the sale process. Ultimately, what was intended as a legacy could become a source of friction and difficulty for the next generation.

46. Most people prefer to own their business spaces. They think that they are lowering expenses and avoiding the stress of rent fluctuations, while at the same time, the value of their property will increase. While this can create stability, it also limits growth. If your business needs to expand, you are confined to the space you own. Renting allows more flexibility— when the business grows, you can move to a larger space; when it contracts, you can downsize without the burden of an owned property. Look around your cities and towns and you will notice so many old shops and offices that haven't grown. It's because they created a comfort zone around themselves that they couldn't escape.

47. Buy real estate for consumption. If you desire a house, a vacation home or a farmhouse—then go

ahead. But think twice about your exit plan before investing in real estate. Split your objectives. Separate properties for personal consumption from those for investment. Don't confuse the two.

"Real estate is a golden prison."

Chapter – 08

THE PRICE OF PLENTY

Once upon a time in the lively kingdom of Dunbridge, King Ferdinand had a big idea to end poverty. He thought, "What if we give lots of coins to the poor? They'll be rich, and everyone will be happy!"

Excited, the king ordered the royal mint to make heaps of shiny new coins. Bags of coins were handed out to the people, and at first, everyone was thrilled. Markets were bustling, and the poor felt like they hit the jackpot.

But here's where the trouble began. With so many coins around, people started wanting more stuff. The baker thought, "I can charge more for my bread now." The blacksmith and the vegetable seller had the same idea. Suddenly, everything costs more coins than before.

People were confused. "Why is everything so expensive now?" they wondered. The problem was that when there's too much money, prices go up, and you need more money to buy the same things.

The rich, who had built a certain lifestyle over the years, could still afford a comfortable life but were unhappy to let go of the luxuries they were now used to. They wanted even fancier things, but couldn't afford to. Everyone wanted more, and that made prices go even higher.

King Ferdinand noticed the confusion and frustration among his people. He scratched his head, realising his plan had backfired. "I wanted to help, but I made things worse," he admitted to himself. So, the king gathered his helpers and said, "We need to fix this."

Slowly, the kingdom learned. People started being careful with their coins, and the prices in the markets settled down.

Could you keep your lifestyle intact as prices rise? Or would you fall behind, struggling to catch up?

Points to Ponder:

48. Inflation is the rise in the general price level of goods and services. If our investments are not growing at a rate higher than inflation, we are essentially losing money each passing year. The trick to overcome the hurdle of inflation while investing is to look at the true value of money and not its face value. This is the mistake King Ferdinand made. He only considered the price of the money he was going to bring into the market but forgot about its purchasing power.

49. When we consider investing, we usually consider only the amount we're investing and the amount we will be receiving in return. It's essential to remember that our post-tax investment returns should outpace the inflation rate. Taxes can eat into our earnings, impacting the actual growth of our wealth. This is something we often overlook when investing in FDs.

So, it's not just about the advertised returns; we need to ensure that what's left after taxes beats inflation. This approach protects our money from losing value over time, securing our financial future more effectively.

50. Any time our insurance reaches maturity, we are rarely happy with our payout. Why is that? This is because there is not much difference in the purchasing value of the money that we invested as premiums in the earlier years and the purchasing value of the money we received in return. For instance, we invest in a scheme that demands a lakh for which you will receive Rs two lakh: ten years down the line. But what is the true value of Rs two lakh after ten years? Will it have the same purchasing power that it does now? It won't. We often fall for these tricks when we buy insurance policies or bonds that promise to double our money in an 'x' number of years.

51. Devaluation of currency is another factor that you need to consider when planning your expenses, especially if you're looking at goals that are international in nature, be it wanting to educate your children abroad or retire abroad sometime in the future. This is also true for people whose country of income is different from their country of residence or expenditure.

"Overtake inflation otherwise inflation will overtake you."

Chapter – 09

NEEDS TO DREAM

Nikhil grew up in Thiruvananthapuram, a city embraced by the sea. His childhood was coloured by frequent trips to Kovalam, where the sound of crashing waves became a symphony to his ears. It was on the shores of Lighthouse Beach that his love affair with surfing began.

At the age of 16, Nikhil paddled out into the shallow waters and discovered the exhilarating thrill of riding waves. By 18, he was a proficient surfer, intimately acquainted with the ebb and flow of the ocean at Lighthouse Beach. Even during college in Manipal, Nikhil's passion for surfing remained undiminished. During breaks from his studies, he would regularly drive down for an hour to Mulki, where he found another surf spot.

Upon graduating and securing a job, Nikhil's longing for the sea only intensified. Now armed with a steady income, he bought his own gear and surfing board and enrolled himself in an indoor surfing club in the city. He even sought out new surfing destinations. In his early twenties, he often took trips to Pondicherry during summers, to seek the adrenaline rush of surfing.

As years passed and his career flourished, Nikhil's passions soared. He kept ticking places off his list. He had now explored the waters of Fiji, Bali, and the Maldives, each wave adding to his memories. But this wasn't enough for Nikhil.

Having now become too familiar with the waves of Southeast Asia, Nikhil wanted to aim higher. His next goal was conquering the legendary North Shore of Oahu, Hawaii. The North Shore of Oahu holds a revered place in the surfing world, beckoning enthusiasts from across the globe. The only problem was that it had only a few, very exclusive and expensive surfing resorts.

Do you think Nikhil would choose to plan a trip to Oahu? Is he wrong in wanting to challenge himself a step further?

Points to Ponder:

52. Governments provide figures guiding our financial decisions. The information we have in hand is that general inflation occurs at the pace of 4 to 6% annually. But these figures are not the full picture. They only focus on basic necessities like *roti*, *kapda* and *makaan*, but don't account for our evolving tastes and desires. Though designed to assist us in sustaining our current lifestyle, they fail to consider a fundamental aspect of human nature—the perpetual desire for growth.

53. The often-overlooked factor that can skew our understanding of our financial needs is lifestyle inflation. Your personal inflation rate changes depending on your living choices. Are you consuming simple *rotis* at home or are you enjoying fancy breads, pastas and pizzas at high-end restaurants? If you fall ill, would you prefer the services of a government hospital, or does a private one align more closely with your expectations? Likewise, reflect on your own educational experiences. Is your child attending the same school as you did? Don't you have higher aspirations for your life and academics?

54. Just like Nikhil constantly upgraded his passion for surfing, do you not want to do the same with your life? It's natural to want to improve our quality of life. That's why we work so hard to earn. Our habits dictate that we elevate our standards, and failure to do so can lead to stagnation and challenges. It's essential to be aware of its impact on our finances. Ignoring it can lead to skewed financial planning. If we plan our financial goals based only on the inflation percentage, we risk missing out on the pleasures of life that go beyond the essentials.

55. We must redefine our approach to understanding inflation. If you create your goals based on the government's inflation rates, you will end up chasing the wrong numbers. Take a closer look at your total annual expenses over the past three to five years. Evaluate the increase in your total expenses. This will

reveal the rate at which your lifestyle is truly evolving. You will see that your expenses are increasing at a significantly higher rate than the government-prescribed 6%. Your personal inflation will typically range between 10 to 15%. And this is the rate you need to adhere to.

"Inflation is a distraction, lifestyle inflation is the actual truth."

Chapter – 10

WISDOM OF TIME

In a prosperous kingdom, there reigned a king known for his prowess in chess. His ego was as vast as his kingdom, and he would challenge every skilled chess player who dared to cross his path. One day, an old sage, humble and unassuming, passed through the kingdom. The king, driven by his competitive nature, promptly challenged the old sage to a game.

The sage, however, refused to engage in the chess match. Instead, he proposed a peculiar wager. "I ask for a simple offering," said the sage. "One grain of rice for the first square of the chessboard, and then double that amount for each succeeding square until we reach the 64th square."

Amused by what he perceived as the sage's naivete, the king agreed, thinking he was making a generous offer. Little did he know the profound implications of compounding.

The game commenced, and as the days progressed, so did the number of grains of rice owed to the sage. On the first day, a single grain; on the second, two grains; on the third, four grains, and so forth. The compounding effect began to reveal its power.

After two weeks, the sage had accumulated a meagre amount—equivalent to a cup of rice. The king, initially dismissive, grew slightly uneasy. By the third week, the sage's bounty amounted to a sack of rice. Frustration crept into the king's mind, but the sage persisted.

As the game reached the 40th or 41st square, the king faced an astonishing realisation. To fulfil his end of the bargain, he would need to deliver an amount of rice equivalent to the value of his entire kingdom and more. The once-confident king now grappled with the consequences of underestimating the power of compounding.

Could you imagine a single grain of rice growing into such a huge quantity? Doesn't it make you think about the potential of small things multiplying over time?

Points to Ponder:

56. Albert Einstein once described compound interest as the eighth wonder of the world, a force that could work for or against us depending on our understanding. It's the concept of "interest on interest," where each year's interest is calculated on the cumulative sum of the principal and interest from the previous year. This financial phenomenon has the potential to transform small investments into substantial wealth over time.

57. Many investors make the mistake of withdrawing their funds as soon as they start seeing higher returns. True compounding only begins after you have given your investment some years in the stock market. Even traditional products like PPF (Public Provident Fund) and insurance worked wonders in 20 years. If a 6-8% compounding rate can give you such returns in 20 years, envision the potential of 12-15% compounding over the same period. It can be a game-changer for you. That initial higher return only means that your money has completed its incubation period and it is now time to gain actual high returns. That is the beauty of compound interest.

58. Let's take the business world as an example. People who've been in business for 10, 40, or even 100 years, people with "old money" often have more wealth than people with recent businesses, even if they aren't as innovative or growing at the rate of new businesses. They don't always get rich from doing extraordinary things. It's more about consistently making money over time. Even if it's just a decent amount, it adds up over generations. That is what compounding is. Start early so you have more time to compound your wealth.

59. The same idea applies even to careers. If you stick to one profession for a long time, you become an expert and successful. Your knowledge compounds. You keep learning and getting better at your job. You don't need to do something amazing to become

successful; it's about steadily gaining expertise over time.

60. So, in business, professions and investing, the key is the time you put in and the steady growth it brings. The lesson here is clear: patience and a long-term perspective are essential components of unlocking the true potential of compound interest.

"The longer you wait, the bigger the rewards."

Chapter – 11

TRUE INVESTMENT VALUE

The Thomas family, exhausted but jubilant after a spirited football match, decided to cap the day with a family dinner at their local pizzeria. The aroma of freshly baked pizza crusts and savoury toppings filled the air as they settled into a cosy corner booth.

"Mom, Dad, I'm starving!" exclaimed Daniel, the youngest Thomas, his eyes eagerly scanning the menu. Emily, his sister, nodded in agreement. "Yeah, and after that game, I could eat a whole pizza by myself!"

The parents shared a knowing glance, fully aware of the ravenous hunger that often follows strenuous physical activity. "How about we get an 8-inch pizza for each of you to share?" he suggested. However, Daniel had other plans. "No way, Dad!" objected Daniel. "Let's each get our own 4-inch pizza!"

Mrs. Thomas raised an eyebrow. "If you're hungry enough, I guess we could."

"That's what I thought too, Mom," added Emily. "But we just learned about areas and volumes in the school. Trust me; ordering an 8-inch pizza to share would be better. It has more volume than two 4-inch pizzas combined!"

She went on to explain the maths to them with enthusiasm, "In school, we learned how to calculate the area of a circle." She quickly took the tissue papers on the table and sketched out the calculations on them. "They might seem like the same size if you look only at the numbers, but if you use the correct formula, you'll realise that the volume of one 8-inch pizza is double compared to two 4-inch pizzas!"

"Try drawing one big circle and two smaller circles inside it! Isn't there still so much space left?" she continued explaining.

Mr Thomas looked at her calculations and realised that she was right! He had failed to recognise this even though he knew the formula. With a chuckle, he admitted, "Well, it seems we have budding mathematicians in the family. Let's go for the 8-inch pizza to share!"

Ever assumed two 4-inch pizzas equal an 8-inch one? When have you misjudged value by just looking at the numbers?

Points to Ponder:

61. Like Mr and Mrs. Thomas, we also tend to calculate our returns on the face value of numbers instead of looking at the actual maths behind the growth. This is because we evaluate our investment decisions based on the number of times our investment has grown. Let's say your grandfather bought a piece of land

50 years ago for ₹25000 and the price of that land is ₹1 crore today. You will take pride in the investment and assume that it was a fantastic investment because its market value is now 400 times what it used to be. However, the fallacy lies in assuming that our returns are as straightforward 400 times. To truly understand the dynamics of our investment performance, we must consider the time value of money.

62. The Compound Annual Growth Rate (CAGR) Formula becomes a vital tool in deciphering the actual growth of our investments, particularly about the amount of time we have put into them. This is especially important when it comes to evaluating long-term investments like gold, real estate and insurance that require long periods to show returns. It tells you if the time you put in is worth the return you'll be getting. Calculating the CAGR yourself might be complex but a simple web search will show you a wide array of calculators that make your job so much easier.

63. Applying this formula to our earlier example will reveal a more realistic growth rate of only 12.73%. While this can be a respectable percentage, other instruments could have provided higher returns. This sheds light on the fact that the appreciation in market price is not a direct representation of our actual returns. As the property value increases, so does the value of our initial investment, resulting in a lower percentage of real returns than our initial assumption.

64. Another common fallacy that we fall for is insurance policies. Consider an insurance policy where you invest 50k every year for ten years (a total of 5 lakhs), and then you get 50k every year for the next 30 years (a total of 15 lakhs. You might think you are getting three times the money you have invested, but the actual CAGR is only 6.4%, which barely crosses the personal inflation percentages.

65. One often overlooked aspect in return calculations is the impact of external taxes. Consider a Fixed Deposit (FD) that claims to offer a 7.5% return. However, this figure fails to account for the taxes deducted annually. FDs are taxed at 30%, so the actual return you're making in terms of in-hand money is only 5.25%.

66. Equity has management fees, real estate accrues maintenance costs, and jewellery comes with making charges. All of these additional expenses need to be subtracted from your gross return to give you your actual net return. The mistake we make is that we forget about these expenses, look only at the gross returns and get happy with the wrong numbers. We need to break out from these myths and look at the true value of our investments.

67. When comparing any two assets, one must compare them like an apple to an apple. This means that you need to use the same parameters to judge the two assets. You wouldn't judge oranges and apples with the same parameters. Similarly, if one product

promises a certain CAGR in 5 years and another promises a higher CAGR in 10 years, then you can't compare the two. They need to both have similar parameters for you to pick which one's better.

"Wrong metrics lead to illusions, not solutions."

Chapter – 12

LOCKED WEALTH

Have you heard of the play, *The Merchant of Venice* by William Shakespeare? In the play, there is a character named Antonio, a wealthy merchant residing in Venice. Antonio was known for his generosity and his willingness to help his friends, but little did he know that his financial decisions would soon put him in a precarious situation.

Antonio had invested a significant portion of his wealth in ventures overseas, primarily in merchant ships. While his ventures were usually profitable, there were inherent risks associated with international trade during those times.

One day, his close friend Bassanio approached him. Bassanio, a young Venetian nobleman, was deeply in love with the beautiful heiress Portia but lacked the financial means to court her. He sought Antonio's help to fund his courtship. Antonio couldn't turn away from his dear friend. However, most of his wealth was tied up overseas in his trading ships, and he had limited cash on hand. To help Bassanio, Antonio decided to borrow money from the Jewish moneylender Shylock.

Shylock, aware of Antonio's financial condition and harbouring a deep-seated grudge against him, proposed a unique and seemingly harmless agreement: if Antonio failed to repay the loan within three months, Shylock would be entitled to a pound of Antonio's flesh. Unaware of the potential consequences, Antonio agreed to the terms, confident that his ships would return with profitable goods, allowing him to repay the loan well within the agreed-upon time frame.

As the story unfolded, Antonio's ships faced further delays, and he found himself unable to fulfil his financial obligations. The three-month deadline approached rapidly, and Antonio faced the grim prospect of losing a pound of his own flesh.

In the end though, Portia, posing as a legal expert, cleverly argues that while Shylock was entitled to a pound of Antonio's flesh, the agreement did not permit the shedding of blood. She highlighted this oversight and contended that any bloodshed would violate the terms, rendering the contract void. Portia's astute interpretation of the agreement saved Antonio from the severe consequences he could have faced. Antonio's life was fortunately spared, and Shylock was forced to renounce his claim.

Why did Antonio, despite his wealth, end up in debt? How could Antonio have ensured financial stability first?

Points to Ponder:

68. Planning money in a way that lets you access it easily is called "liquidity planning." This means having some money in the bank or easily convertible assets that you can use in case of unexpected expenses or emergencies. We need to have money when we need it.

69. When creating an investment plan, people get so lured by the returns that they completely ignore liquidity planning. But planning your liquidity first can yield you more returns. The longer you can keep your investments untouched, the higher your returns will be. This is why you need to align your liquidity plan in a manner that allows you to deal with all your goals and expenses without having to prematurely pull out your investments.

70. Even when you head out of your house on a daily basis, you ensure you have some amount of disposable money on you, be it cash, card or payment apps. The longer your journey is away from home, the more cash you keep on you. Imagine if you didn't have your wallet on you when you left home, you would constantly feel anxious. Life is the biggest journey. Not having enough liquidity will always leave you too anxious to enjoy it.

71. People make the mistake of investing in locked assets like insurance, bonds, startups and real estate without considering that this might make them

short on liquidity. Always remember that returns with liquidity are always better than returns without liquidity. Making a mistake while planning your liquidity can adversely, even put a dent in your returns.

72. People can also struggle with over-liquidity. Over-liquidity is when we have an excess of funds, either cash or usable money in the bank. This means you are not letting your money grow and work for you. People often choose to put their money in recurring year-long fixed deposits. Having three to six months of your income as an emergency corpus is more than enough. The rest can be invested as per your financial goals.

73. The idea is to find a balance between safe and liquid choices that allow accessibility and investing in some other long-term assets that give you higher returns.

"Prepare first, profit later."

Chapter – 13

TAMING FEAR

Meet Saanvi, a 20-year-old college student who's been dealing with a fear of water all her life. This fear, known as aquaphobia, has made her avoid anything related to water like the plague. Even though her friends were all water enthusiasts, she couldn't bring herself to learn how to swim or enjoy water activities. It's like water was her biggest nightmare.

However, things changed when she agreed to go on a trip to Goa with her adventurous buddies. They decided to spend the day at a secluded beach, all excited about swimming and playing in the water. They tried to convince Saanvi to join them. "The water's shallow here, you'll be safe," they said, but her fear ran deep. Even ankle-deep water seemed risky and terrifying. She longed to have fun with her friends, but fear held her back. She had two choices, either to stay completely away from water or learn to be friendly with it. She chose the latter.

After returning to Delhi, Saanvi decided it was time to face her fear. She enrolled in swimming lessons at her college. At first, just the sight of a 4-foot pool gave her shivers. However, her instructor was incredibly patient and understanding, guiding her through the process step by step, and helping her build confidence.

As months passed, a remarkable transformation occurred. Her fear of water slowly faded away, replaced by a newfound sense of empowerment. Saanvi went from being a timid non-swimmer to a confident and skilled swimmer. She had conquered her deepest fears with unwavering determination.

When her friends proposed another adventure at a lake house, Saanvi needed no convincing. Without a second thought, she packed her swimsuit and felt an overwhelming sense of excitement and anticipation.

At the lake house, Saanvi took a deep breath and carefully stepped into the lake. The cool water first touched her toes, and in that moment, she felt a surge of bravery. Encouraged, she ventured further, wading into the depths and then gracefully swimming alongside her friends.

Why are the waters less intimidating now? How and why did Saanvi overcome her initial fear?

Points to Ponder:

74. Just as Saanvi had to figure out her fear of water, we all need to think about our attitude towards financial risk, often referred to as our 'risk appetite.' Some people are like daredevil swimmers, jumping into deep waters, while others prefer to stick to the shallow end. Similarly, in the financial world, some folks are comfortable with high-risk investments that

might bring big rewards, while others like to play it safe with low-risk options.

75. Now, think about how Saanvi had to assess her swimming skills to deal with her fear of water, which is her risk capacity. The better her swimming skills became, the more confident she felt in deeper waters. In the world of finance, you've got to assess your financial situation. That means looking at your goals, how long you've got to achieve them, and what you can afford to invest without putting your financial security in danger. This assessment helps you decide how much financial risk you can comfortably handle.

76. You've also got to understand your risk tolerance. It is all about how calm you can stay when things get a bit rocky. Saanvi developed the tolerance to stay calm in deep water.

77. Before you dive into any investment, it's a smart move to educate yourself about different investment options. Stocks, bonds, real estate—there are lots of choices, and each comes with its own level of risk. For Saanvi, life without swimming was okay but learning swimming changed it completely. Similarly, we may be comfortable with traditional investments like FDs, gold, and real estate, but stepping out of our comfort zone and learning about other instruments of investment like equity can help us make informed decisions.

78. The more time Saanvi spent in water, the less risky it seemed to her. Similarly, equity itself is not risky, not spending enough time with it makes it risky. Learning can help us bring down this risk. We limit our choices when we don't have enough knowledge. The willingness to take risks and building a risk tolerance can create a significant difference in our financial portfolio.

79. Start with safer options, get advice from experts, read up on finance, and slowly build your expertise. As your confidence grows, you can wade into deeper waters, just like Saanvi did when she confidently swam alongside her friends. The lesson here is that just as Saanvi learned to conquer her fear, you can master the art of managing financial risks and sail through the unpredictable waves of finance with confidence.

80. Although Saanvi had learned how to swim, she was still cautious because the lake was a different environment. Similarly, understanding market behaviour and adapting accordingly is crucial for successful investing. The market operates independently and does not respond to individual preferences or desires. By observing trends and adjusting your strategies to align with market conditions, you can make more informed decisions and improve your chances of achieving favourable outcomes.

81. Achieving your financial goal is more important. If your current investment strategy is not helping you achieve your goal then you are left with two choices: You can either forget your goal or you can switch to a different strategy.

"Learn to risk or risk growth"

Chapter – 14

WORK SMARTER, NOT HARDER

Amidst the hilly scenery of Uttarakhand, in a quaint village, there lived a strong woodcutter. Eager to put his skills to good use, he approached the local timber merchant, who was known for paying his employees generously and providing them with good working conditions.

The timber merchant readily gave him a job. He handed him a shiny new axe and guided him to a lush area where he could fall trees. The new axe filled the woodcutter with determination. On the first day, he swung his axe with precision and vigour, managing to bring down a total of eighteen trees by the end of the day. The boss, impressed, congratulated him, saying, "Keep up the excellent work!"

Feeling proud of himself after hearing the praise, the woodcutter approached the second day with renewed enthusiasm, determined to outdo his previous performance. However, to his dismay, he could only fall fifteen trees. Undeterred, he resolved to push himself harder on the third day, but his efforts yielded only ten fallen trees. The trend continued, and with each passing day, there was a decline in the woodcutter's productivity.

Perplexed and disheartened, the woodcutter began to doubt his strength. He approached the boss with an apology, expressing his confusion about the sudden decline in his performance. "I must be losing my strength," the woodcutter lamented. The wise boss, rather than scolding him, calmly inquired, "When was the last time you sharpened your axe?"

The woodcutter, taken aback, confessed, "Sharpen? I've had no time to sharpen my axe. I have been so busy trying to cut down trees."

With a knowing smile, the boss explained, "Your strength is not the issue; it's the sharpness of your tool. An axe loses its sharpness over time, you have to regularly sharpen it. It might take some time, but it makes it efficient and ensures that your hard work doesn't go in vain."

How do you think the story relates to your financial mindset? Do you think the boss' advice was correct?

Points to Ponder:

82. Most people put all their time and energy into earning money. However, they get so caught up in the grind, that they often forget to set aside some time to actually manage it.

83. Money is a tool, just like the woodcutter's axe. Just like the woodcutter needed to sharpen his axe to make full use of his strength and power, we too

need to invest and grow our money to ensure that it doesn't lose its value. Spending time managing your money is as important as the time you spend earning it.

84. When it comes to earning money, we are okay with getting up in the wee hours of the morning or even staying back late. But we find it difficult to do the same for managing our money. We refuse to take out even a couple of hours a week from our busy schedules for wealth management.

85. Sometimes we become overconfident about earning money just like the woodcutter was overconfident in his strength. We then start believing that others managing money are fools wasting their time, which is not true at all.

86. Taking the time to learn about managing money doesn't mean you have to become a financial expert. It means building adequate knowledge that prevents you from being taken advantage of.

87. Just like the timber merchant guided the woodcutter to sharpen the sword, you need a mentor. Seeking guidance can help simplify the process of money management and ensure that you are making the right choices for your future. Don't let ignorance be an excuse to avoid investing.

"Earning to get rich; manage to stay wealthy."

Chapter – 15

SHIFTING PRIORITIES

Anika worked hard her entire life to become a lawyer. At 30, she is now a successful corporate lawyer in Mumbai and has climbed the ranks to become a junior partner at one of the country's most prestigious law firms. Her work was demanding, but it came with its rewards. Her days were filled with high-stakes negotiations and intricate legal battles involving some of the biggest corporate giants. The financial fruits of her labour were substantial, and she found herself with an income that far exceeded that of most people her age.

Since her early twenties, Anika had been diligently investing a small but fixed amount of a couple of thousand rupees. Her investments were handled by her father's friend who was an insurance agent back in her hometown, Jabalpur. He had been helping her family with their investments for years and like her father, she also naturally started entrusting her money with him. However, with her significant increase in income, a friend suggested that she reconsider her investment strategy. The advice was to increase her investment to at least ₹50,000, a proportionate amount to her elevated earnings. The idea lingered in her mind, and she decided to seek guidance.

Anika had once faced losses because of an investment mistake, and so she decided to be extra thorough this time. She tried doing her research on the Internet, but the numbers seemed too complex, and she could not make sense of the financial jargon. So, she approached her senior colleagues, seeking advice on the potential investment shift. She also discussed it with her parents. Her father suggested that she come back to Jabalpur for a couple of days to meet them and also discuss the investment with his friend in person. Anika took the matter seriously; after all, it was an important decision that could shape her financial future. However, amidst the busy days at the law firm, weeks turned into months, and Anika was still grappling with the decision.

Around the same time, her car broke down. It was her father's old car that he had decided to give her when she moved to Mumbai. She called him up and told him that the mechanic had suggested that changing her car would be a more economical decision. After informing her father, she started researching various models on the internet. Initially, she was flustered by all the automobile technicalities, but after a couple of hours of dedicated research, the numbers started making sense, her interest piqued and soon she was well versed with torque, RPM, mileage and size.

She did her research on various cars and the best dealers around her and finally decided on the car of her dreams, a compact luxury SUV that would help her navigate the narrow, bumpy roads of the city. She found the best dealer in her area who offered her a price close to Rs 30 lakh. After a test drive that left her exhilarated, Anika made the swift decision to buy it. However, the red colour that she had liked wasn't available. A quick search helped her find a dealer in Pune who had the car ready and she decided to book it. Rather than dipping into her savings, she opted for a car loan to finance the purchase, which meant she had to pay a down payment of ₹8 lakh and at least Rs 50,000 every month as EMI.

Restless and excited, Anika could not stop herself from going down to Pune with her friends to bring the car home. They celebrated and drove the car back to Mumbai full of excitement, enjoying the scenic views. In less than three days, the sleek SUV car had become part of her daily routine, accompanying her to the law firm every morning. The luxury car served as a symbol of her hard work and success, a tangible reward for the long hours and sleepless nights she had dedicated to her career.

What is the difference in Anika's attitudes towards spending and investing? Why do you think that is?

Points to Ponder:

88. Understanding certain behavioural patterns is crucial for cultivating a healthier financial mindset. For instance, spending is easy. Since it is money that we have earned, we want to be responsible for the way it is spent and we enjoy our spending power. It takes just five minutes to decide to splurge on a night out

with friends, but when it comes to investing the same amount, suddenly time stretches to five months. The ease with which we spend is because we crave the immediate satisfaction it provides. Saving, on the other hand, requires foresight, and a commitment to delayed gratification which we lack the patience for.

89. When it comes to investments, we are looking to pass on the responsibility to someone else. We feel the need to collectively discuss and deliberate the decision with family, friends, financial advisors, and perhaps even professionals like chartered accountants. It's not just an individual decision any more. But when it's spending, we take pride in our ability to spend and make our own decisions. No one likes to ask for advice on every small expenditure.

90. Research behaviours also differ when it comes to spending versus investing. We're super careful when buying everyday household items or things we want. We compare, we read reviews, and we take our time. But, oddly enough, when it comes to investing— you know, the important stuff—we often skip the careful part. Maybe it's because we're hoping for quick profits or because the whole finance world seems too confusing. Take Anika for example, who was very active when it came to researching her new car but found herself in a pickle when it came to her investments.

91. Past financial setbacks can leave a lasting impact on our financial mindset. We find solace in spending,

even if there is no guarantee that it results in a positive experience. A bad expense once made, is a loss forever. But, when it comes to investing, even the worst investment, will give us a portion of our money back. Despite knowing this fact, we still stay away from investments.

92. The core challenge lies in our prioritisation. Anika couldn't find the time to go down to Jabalpur and discuss her investments with her father but when it came to buying her car, she dropped all her meetings and drove down to Pune. Shifting from 'I want it now' to 'I'll benefit later' is essential for building sustainable wealth.

93. With time, as our income grows, so do our spending and expenses. Anika, who up until then was driving her father's old car, decided to buy a luxury car because she could now afford it. Ideally, our expenses need to grow slower than our income, but that rarely happens. In fact, it's vice versa. Our expenses grow faster than our income does. And so, just as we increase our spending, we need to raise our investment as our income grows.

94. Anika's story shows us how spending on things we desire is easy and quick, giving us instant joy. On the other hand, when it comes to investing the same amount of money for the future, we tend to think more, discuss more, and invest less. Understanding these differences helps us rethink our priorities, challenge our fears, and see the value in making

investments that can benefit us in the long run. Spending makes us happy, investing does not.

"Spending is easy; saving is difficult."

Chapter – 16

GROWTH ON AUTOPILOT

Aahana, a passionate fashion designer in Mumbai, had always dreamed of giving her family home in Juhu a fresh, modern look that reflected her style. The house, a family treasure for generations, had grown old and outdated. But Aahana's fashion business was booming, and her dream of transforming her home was always pushed aside.

Aahana was a hard worker, dedicating herself to building her fashion brand. Her days were filled with dealing with clients, designing clothes, selecting fabrics, managing collections, talking to dealers, stocking her store, and paying bills. She also had family responsibilities, like caring for her ageing parents and taking them to medical appointments.

As her fashion business continued to grow, Aahana felt overwhelmed and found it hard to make time for her dream. Her home project seemed impossible. Aahana understood that she couldn't do everything on her own. To create more time for herself, she decided to delegate some tasks to others.

First, she hired a capable manager for her boutique, someone who knew the fashion industry well. This manager handled the material supply, ensuring her store always had the latest fabrics and accessories. He also ensured that the customers got great service when she wasn't around. Aahana didn't have to worry about supplies or negotiations anymore. Next, she created a system to follow when it came to her boutique's monthly bills. She gave the manager a checklist of things to take care of at the end of every month that he adhered to. This freed her from the hassles of dealing with these payments. With this support, Aahana finally had time for her personal life and her home project.

Aahana's decision to automate and delegate business tasks gave her control over her time. She could now work on her personal dream—transforming her family house as well as focus more on expanding her business. As she started working on her home, Aahana found balance and fulfilment.

Did Aahana make the right choice with automation and delegation? How can you apply these strategies for personal and financial gain?

Points to Ponder:

95. In the journey to developing a financial mindset that nurtures growth and security, we often find ourselves at a crossroads when it comes to financial tasks like saving, investing, paying bills, EMIs, insurance premiums, rent etc. Just like Aahana, we must understand the importance of delegation in our personal finances. The key to growth is discipline and

to maintain discipline, we either dedicate ourselves to our tasks or delegate the tasks to someone and automate them.

96. Your brain has to handle a staggering 35,000 decisions each day, spanning from the most trivial to the most complex. Money decisions fall into the latter category. Crunching numbers is difficult and as a result, our brains tend to procrastinate when it comes to investment choices. Which is why not making the decisions is the easiest decision. Automating and delegating your financial decisions can be a game-changer.

97. Just as we now automate monthly payments like EMIs, think about automating all your financial tasks. Deciding when and where to invest a portion of your earnings every time can be a daunting task. But if a fixed portion of your earnings is automatically diverted from your bank account into various investment streams the process becomes a breeze.

98. From business commitments to personal obligations, we have a list of excuses that often get in the way of managing our finances. When your brain is occupied with all these things, financial planning takes a backseat and you tend to postpone your investment decisions. This is precisely why delegation is essential. Find someone who ensures that, irrespective of the numerous uncertainties and distractions life throws your way, your financial future remains secure.

99. The journey of wealth creation is a marathon, not a sprint. But managing money consistently is next to impossible. Will you have the discipline to invest consistently every month for the rest of your life? Automation removes the burden of consistency and ensures that your money works for you, year after year, without fail.

"Automation is the first step to wealth creation."

Chapter – 17

GOAL FIRST, STRATEGY NEXT

Harsh, Shaunak, and Hriday, buddies from way back in school, had grown up to follow their dreams. Harsh was busy running his family's business based in Chandigarh, Shaunak was teaching economics at Delhi University, and Hriday was CEO of a software company in Bangalore. When May rolled around, they decided to take a trip to Shimla for a summer weekend where Hriday's company had a cosy guest house.

Choosing how to get there was a bit of a puzzle. Since they were all busy and lived in different places, they decided it was better for them to travel to the destination separately, as long as they reached the guest house on Friday morning.

Harsh was not fond of road trips. He had once witnessed a life-threatening accident in the hills, which had left him in fear. However, since this was the only option available to him, he chose not to drive down himself and took his driver along.

Shaunak, with plenty of time to spare and a limited budget, thought the train was a great idea. He liked the idea of kicking back and enjoying the views outside the window. He was also looking forward to taking the connecting toy train from Kalka to Shimla. Unfortunately, his train was delayed and he lost his connection, which is why Harsh picked him up on his way and they travelled the rest of the journey together.

Hriday had always been an adventurous person. He especially loved road trips and even owned a four-wheel drive. He had always wanted to drive his car through the Himalayas. Unfortunately, he was swamped with work and had to opt for the quickest route—taking a plane straight to Shimla.

Even though their travel plans were all over the map, they miraculously reached Shimla at the same time. The trio reunited at Hriday's guest house, surrounded by the peaceful mountains.

What made them all happy was that despite their hiccups, they had reached Shimla on time. Shaunak, who wanted to keep it budget-friendly, was all smiles because the train hadn't dented his wallet too much. Harsh, who was fearful of road trips, was happy to have reached Shimla safely. Hriday, always in a race against the clock, was thrilled to get there pronto and not miss any important work meetings.

As the sun dipped behind the mountains, the friends laughed and soaked in the moment, loving the fact that they had each stuck to their individual game plan. They realised that it was reaching the goal that was important. It did not matter how they got to their destination as long as they reached on time, even if it meant going outside their comfort zone. United by their diverse paths, they found joy in being together, making memories against the stunning backdrop of Shimla.

How do Harsh, Shaunak, and Hriday's different travel methods illustrate the idea of 'success at your own pace'? Did their varying journeys have any impact on their destination?

Points to Ponder:

100. In the vast landscape of financial markets, navigating the journey of investing without a clear goal is like setting out on the road without deciding where to go. Consider your financial goals as the roadmap guiding your investment choices. Just as Shaunak chose the train, Harsh took the road, and Hriday opted for the sky, your investment vehicle should align with your financial objectives.

101. Harsh put his discomfort with road travel aside for a bigger goal—spending quality time with his friends. The key is to stay focused on your goal, ensuring that you will reach it, irrespective of what you are comfortable with. Just because you had a bad experience with a certain asset class, does not mean you will always have a bad experience with it. If your goal demands you invest in it, then do it.

102. Time is an important factor when making investments. Shaunak, who had more time on his hands, chose the train. Hriday, on the other hand,

was busy with work and took a flight. Similarly, you need to distinguish between long-term and short-term goals and tailor your investment approach accordingly. Long-term goals, like retirement, require a patient and aggressive investment strategy. Short-term goals like buying a house, may involve more conservative investment strategies.

103. Remember the mantra: what gets measured gets done. Just like Shaunak changed his route based on his needs, you also need to track your progress toward your financial goals regularly. Goal reviewing is crucial. This not only helps you stay accountable but also allows you to make adjustments to your investment strategy as needed.

104. When you only track your returns, you end up taking more risks to achieve a higher return. But when you track your goal, you make sure you achieve it safely and on time. Choose your vehicle wisely. Invest in instruments that resonate with your goals, whether it's building wealth for your children's education, creating a retirement nest egg or leaving a legacy for your future generations. With a clear goal in mind, you won't deviate from your objective, and the path to financial success becomes clearer.

"Focus on the goal, tweak the paths."

Chapter – 18

SHORTCUTS AND SETBACKS

Abhishek and Karan, two childhood friends from Kolkata, had always been inseparable. Their families shared a close bond, and they often embarked on vacations together. This time, they decided to explore a farmhouse near Darjeeling, a picturesque destination known for its serene beauty and vineyards.

Excitement bubbled within them as they set off in two separate cars, one for each family.

Abhishek, known for his steady nature, chose to stick to the familiar highway and main roads, promising a smoother journey. Karan, on the other hand, had left a little later which made him feel impatient and eager to reach their destination as quickly as possible.

On the way, Karan saw an old dusty signboard that said 30 km to Darjeeling, which was much shorter than what Google Maps was showing and would have saved him an hour. Impatience got the best of him, and he made the sudden decision to leave the traffic-packed highway and take the bumpy, dusty back road. After driving for a bumpy but traffic-less ten minutes, the car reached a narrow, winding unpaved edge, and the family's nervousness reached a peak as they realised, they had to navigate the dangerous road with a cliff on one side.

The road was extremely narrow, and unpaved, with no barriers to shield them from the sheer drop.

To make things even more thrilling, the unpaved roads led to a punctured tyre. He had to stop the car and change the punctured tyre which further slowed them down and left Karan exhausted. The detour had turned into a risky gamble, and the line between thrill and danger blurred.

Meanwhile, Abhishek's family continued their steady ride along the well-built highway. The picturesque countryside views and the soft hum of the car engine made the journey comfortable and enjoyable. They even stopped for a leisurely meal on their way. His family chatted and laughed, savouring the scenic route.

Karan finally found himself back on the highway, and in line for the toll, only to find Abhishek and his family a couple of cars behind him. As they reunited, they couldn't help but share their contrasting experiences. Abhishek's family arrived relaxed and ready to start their vacation, with no sign of fatigue. In contrast, Karan's family exited the car dust-covered and dishevelled, their faces etched with exhaustion. They appeared as if they had just emerged from a battlefield, bearing the visible signs of a rough ride that had left them drained and tired.

As they settled in at the farmhouse and began their vacation, Abhishek and Karan shared their stories and laughed about the adventures they had just experienced.

Who made the better choice in your opinion? Was Karan's route worth all the effort and risk?

Points to Ponder:

105. In the world of finance, the human brain is wired for speculation. We crave the thrill, the excitement, the possibility of quick gains, and, perhaps more than anything, the illusion of control. Yet, as illustrated by Karan's journey, speculation often leads to a perilous path, balancing on the edge of thrill and danger.

106. We only tend to take shortcuts when we haven't started our journey on time. The trick to gaining high returns is starting early. If Karan had left early, he wouldn't have felt so rushed to catch up with Abhishek and taken the risky route. Similarly, speculation is also a shortcut that people take when they are too late and do not have the time or patience to wait for long-term rewards.

107. Speculation involves a series of risky transactions, each laden with its own set of dangers. It will only make you money when all these transactions go correctly but the probability of success in all these transactions is exceedingly low compared to the simplicity of long-term investment, which essentially involves only two transactions: buying and holding. A single wrong move in speculation can result in significant losses.

108. A SEBI report from 2022 declared that 9 out of 10 individual traders in 2022 made a loss. Despite this, we still persistently hold the irrational belief that we could be one of the lucky few. We want to believe that although most people make losses, we won't because we aren't unlucky like them. By the time we realise that we are actually unlucky, it is often too late.

109. If speculation did actually make a lot of money, then several successful industrialists and businessmen would have set up their own systems. Why would they put all their time, energy and resources into building their businesses? They could have hired the best of manpower, technology and money to speculate instead. But they chose to build businesses instead.

110. Long-term investing, where money is committed to a specific goal and left for a predefined time, is like taking the smooth and easy highway to a farmhouse. In the end, despite all the risks, Karan only managed to reach a couple of minutes earlier than Abhishek. Similarly, you might even make a profit from speculation, but it won't be significantly higher than long-term returns. Long-term investing may lack the thrill, but it is a safer and surer way to build wealth.

"Short-cuts can cut short your wealth."

Chapter – 19

THE BUSINESS MINDSET

Long, long ago in the small village of Pokhran, there lived a man named Balram. Balram was known throughout the village for his strong arms and even stronger spirit.

The scorching heat dried up the entire village and water was a precious scarcity, especially in the difficult summer months. One day, while tilling his land, Balram's spade struck something hard beneath the soil. Curious, he began to dig deeper, and to his amazement, water gushed forth from the ground. It was a miracle! But Balram was not one to let go of an opportunity. He saw this as a sign from the gods and was determined to uncover the full extent of this blessing.

Balram saw this as an opportunity to alleviate the water woes of his fellow villagers. He wanted to build a business by selling the water from his well to his fellow villages as an extra source of income.

Day after day, Balram laboured tirelessly, digging deeper and deeper into the earth. And with each scoop of soil, he removed, more water flowed from the ground as if the earth itself was offering its bounty to him.

However, Balram's joy was tinged with a deep-seated fear. In the back of his mind, he harboured a belief that drawing too much water from the well would eventually cause it to run dry. He was afraid to consume water before fully digging the well to the bottom. He believed that the more he dug, the more water would appear, and he wanted to ensure that his family had an abundant supply for years to come.

However, on one scorching summer day, the sun beat down mercilessly upon the land, making it impossible for Balram to continue his work. Exhausted and parched, he returned home. His wife informed him that their water supply had run dry. She would have to walk to the nearby river to get water for the house, which would take at least half an hour.

His wife, seeing his plight, suggested that they draw water from the well. Reluctantly, Balram agreed, knowing that he had no other choice. Soon, the family began using two buckets from the well every day, which made Balram anxious about the water levels of the well. He was afraid that all the efforts he had put into digging the well would soon be for nothing.

Do you think taking out two buckets of water daily from the well would dry out the well? Was Balram right in not wanting to touch the water from the well?

Points to Ponder:

111. Keeping your money in safe instruments is like having a stable job: you receive a steady income, but there's a limit to how much you can earn. It's reliable but lacks the potential for substantial growth. Conversely, investing in equity is like running a business. It's riskier, but the potential for profits is massive, and there's no limit to how much you can earn.

112. Even though business holds a higher risk, most businessmen, whether small or big, earn more than they could have working for someone else. If you look around, you'll find that several businessmen earn crores annually, but very few employees earn even a crore a year. So, investing in equity is a risk, but a risk that is worth taking.

113. Balram realised that the more effort he put in, the more bountiful his reward was. The deeper he dug, the more water filled up his well. But this also meant that taking a bucket or two from it every day would not dry it up. Similarly, businessmen understand that their business is like a well, the more money they put into it, the more profit they make. However, this also means that if you regularly pull out a little money from your business, it won't affect it.

114. Every time Balaram took out a bucket of water, the groundwater would automatically adjust itself and

the water level would remain unchanged. Similarly, if you start pulling out money from your business on a regular basis, your business will gradually adjust its operations to accommodate it. It is better to pull out money little by little than have to do it all at once when you are in need. Pulling out water all at once from the well would definitely dry it up.

115. Many small to medium-sized business owners often intertwine their personal finances with the company's, leading to blurred lines and financial instability. What they should do is pull out money from the business and invest it to grow their own separate personal wealth. That way this money can support you even when your business is struggling. Just as Balram's ultimate goal was to provide water for his family, the ultimate goal of running a business is also to provide a good lifestyle for yourself and your family.

116. Another mistake businessmen make is that they believe it is better to invest in their own business than in someone else's. When our own small business can generate so much profit, it is wrong to assume that bigger businesses don't have similar potential. Buying equity is just investing in a business that isn't yours. Think of it like a sleeping partnership. You are earning a steady cut of the profits, without having to oversee the day-to-day working.

117. During tough times in business, we do everything in our power to save our business. We sometimes even invest more money as we are confident that we will overcome the bad times. The same goes for equity. You need to stick with your equity investments even when the market is down. Stay calm and consider putting in more money instead of exiting. By treating your investments like extensions of your business ventures, you can handle ups and downs more easily.

118. The return on an investment product often depends on the time horizon. For instance, a one-year investment may yield lower returns compared to a five or ten-year investment, as the shorter timeframe limits the growth potential. Investments with a lock-in period tend to offer higher returns because they benefit from remaining invested for longer, while more flexible options without a lock-in may offer lower returns due to increased liquidity. It's important to view this dynamic from both sides. When businesses take out loans, someone is investing in them. On the flip side, when we invest, we are providing funds to borrowers who need capital for their businesses. As a borrower, taking money for the short term often isn't useful or profitable. Long-term financing is more beneficial because it allows businesses the time needed to generate returns. As an investor, it's crucial to understand that when you provide funds for a longer term, you're giving the borrower

sufficient time to use that money effectively to generate profits, which in turn benefits your investment. Understanding the terms from both perspectives helps ensure better outcomes for both the borrower and the investor.

119. Understand the balance between risk and reward. Any business has risks associated with it like investments, stocks, and debtors. However, doubling these risks may not lead to double profit margins. High risk doesn't always mean high rewards. That said, keep your expectations in check without lowering them too much.

120. In any business venture, your appetite plays a crucial role. If your vision is small and your profit expectations are limited, it reflects a smaller appetite for success. Take, for instance, the stock market, which holds the potential for growth as high as 100 times your initial investment amount but people exit the market with lower expectations like 10-15%. The challenge often lies in aligning our appetite with this potential.

"The right mindset redefines risk as an opportunity"

Chapter – 20

PAST IS NOT PROOF

In the vibrant streets of old London, lived a brilliant man, Sir Isaac Newton. Yes, this was the genius who figured out why apples fall from trees and other cool things. But our story isn't about his science, it's about his adventures in money matters.

It was the early 18th century, and the South Sea Company was the talk of the town. The company, riding on the wave of speculative fervour, promised unimaginable wealth to those who invested. Newton, with his keen mind, saw an opportunity and entered the market with a substantial sum. The venture proved to be a triumph, and his investment grew manifold. Newton's pockets overflowed with wealth, and he basked in the glow of financial success.

As the South Sea Company's stock continued to soar, Newton's confidence reached new heights. The allure of easy riches clouded his judgement, and he decided to reinvest a substantial portion of his earnings. After all, the past had been kind to him, and the market seemed invincible. Little did he know that the winds of fortune were fickle.

Soon, the bubble burst. The South Sea Company's stock plummeted, leaving investors in financial ruin.

Newton's once-flourishing portfolio dwindled to a fraction of its former glory. The very man who had deciphered the laws of motion found himself in the grip of financial gravity.

Devastated and shaken, Newton made a grave error—one that would haunt him for years to come. Frustrated by the sudden turn of events, he decided to exit the financial world altogether. The man who had redefined physics for generations resolved to abandon the intricate dance of the stock market.

Years passed, and Newton's intellect remained unmatched, but his financial acumen lay dormant. He missed out on countless opportunities, fearful of the unpredictable nature of the markets. The past, which had once been his ally, became a formidable adversary, a ghost that haunted his every financial decision.

What mistakes did Newton make? Do you think he made the right decision by completely opting out of the financial markets?

Points to Ponder:

121. When it comes to investing and finance, it's easy to fall into the trap of believing that past success is a surefire predictor of future gains. Not just that, we also avoid investments that have shown negative results in the past. Financial markets, though, are not bound by a script. There is no guarantee that

what worked before will work again and on the contrary, something that failed in the past might work this time around. Markets, you see, learn and adapt and rarely repeat the same mistakes.

122. Experienced investors take into consideration several complex numbers, statistics and ratios before making a decision. Constructing a sound financial portfolio requires us to do the same. Unfortunately, whether you're dealing with a financial professional or consulting a Fintech website, historical performance is often the primary selling point. We seek comfort in what we can comprehend, and past returns seem like a simple parameter. However, this oversimplification blinds us to the intricacies of the financial landscape.

123. Markets move in a constant wave pattern. It is considered wise to enter into any asset class when the past return has been dark and murky for a while, because this may be the turning point from which profits will soon arise. On the other hand, very good past returns mean that the asset has been performing consistently for many years and might reach its peak and see a reversal. Newton made the same mistake. Overpowered by the greed and thrill of having made a profit, he put his money back into a stock that was close to reaching its peak. Had he not been excited by the past returns, he would have enjoyed the profits he had initially made by cashing out on time.

124. Historical returns should not be taken as gospel; they may not faithfully replicate in the future. Look at the potential future instead. Isaac Newton's financial journey serves as a reminder that even the brightest minds can stumble in the financial world.

"Past performance does not define future returns."

Chapter – 21

RIDE THE RISK

Mahir lived with his parents in Ahmedabad, a busy city where driving often led to stress. He'd often find himself driving them around, but it wasn't always smooth sailing. His dad, especially, had a knack for backseat driving and wouldn't stop nagging him.

One time, they were headed to a wedding in Baroda. Mahir got ready on time, but his parents were running late. They had an hour and a half to cover a journey typically taking two which made his dad anxious as they navigated through the city's traffic, Mahir drove slowly and cautiously. But his dad kept pushing him to go faster, which only frustrated Mahir more.

"Mahir, can't you go any faster?" his father's voice piped up from the backseat, laced with frustration. "We're going to be late!"

Mahir let out a sigh, glancing briefly at his father through the rearview mirror. "Papa, I'm trying my best here," he replied, his tone strained with the effort of patience. "But speeding up in this traffic isn't safe. We'll get there, I promise."

His mother, sitting beside him, reached out to pat his hand reassuringly. "He's right, dear. Let him drive."

As they finally broke free from the city's grip and hit the open highway, Mahir felt a sense of relief wash over him. He eased his foot down on the accelerator, the car picking up speed smoothly. Mahir sped up to about 120 km/hr, but his moment of peace was short-lived as his father's voice pierced the silence once again. "Mahir, slow down! You're going too fast!"

Mahir suppressed a sigh, his grip on the wheel tightening.

"Papa, we're still within the speed limit," he said, his voice tinged with exasperation. "And the expressway is safe. There's hardly any traffic here. We'll make it on time, I promise."

"Just slow down the car!" Mahir's father exclaimed.

Exasperated, Mahir slowed down the car to 80km/hr. Despite the bickering, they arrived at the wedding. They were a tad behind schedule like Mahir had predicted, but that was okay. Relieved, Mahir parked the car, feeling a sense of accomplishment despite the bumpy journey.

Whose approach do you think would have brought them to Baroda safely and on time? Whose approach was riskier, Mahir's or his father's?

Points to Ponder:

125. Just as our approaches to short and long-distance trips are different, the same goes for investments.

The longer the duration of your goal, the more aggressive you can be with your approach because distance discounts risk and the shorter the distance, the safer you need to play it. But we tend to inverse this instead.

126. When it comes to shorter distances, driving fast on a busy street will increase the probability of an accident. We are aware of this and drive slowly when travelling within the city but when it comes to investing in the short term, we get lured by a couple of extra percent in returns and end up taking more risk.

127. Driving slowly on highways where you know the safe speed limit is a lot higher will only delay your goals. Investing in conservative instruments for the long term may never take you to your goal. Mahir ended up slowing down on the highway because of his father and they ended up reaching late. This would be fine for a wedding but when it comes to your financial goals that's not the case.

128. In the same way, it's crucial to recognise that any investment above the risk-free rate involves some degree of risk. Initially, when seat belts were introduced in cars for safety purposes, they led to more automobile accidents instead. This was because the seatbelt created an illusion of absolute safety leading people to drive riskier than before. Fixed-income products like fixed deposits and bonds are known for being "safe." Under this

illusion of safety, we end up taking more risks and investing in junk companies.

129. Nothing is free and seeking safety also comes at a cost, and that cost is opportunity—the opportunity to yield higher returns. The opportunity cost of seeking safety can be substantial, potentially limiting the growth of your money, just like Mahir slowed down on the highway due to his father's concerns, which resulted in them being late.

130. Investing out of a sense of duty or societal pressure can cloud your judgment. Like Mahir, who remained undeterred by the constant nagging of his father, you need to approach investment decisions with a rational and calm mindset. Our thinking and perception are influenced by the societal environment we inhabit. The constant flow of information, especially through social media, can create a herd mentality, compelling us to follow trends without thorough consideration.

131. Success or failure in investments is a personal responsibility that goes beyond mere intelligence. It demands patience and emotional control, but most importantly it requires one to stick to the basics. People lack the discipline and implementation for consistent investment which is why they then take unnecessary risks to catch up to their goals. If you stick to the two rules mentioned above, you will increase your rewards while decreasing your risks.

If Mahir's father had not been late and left on time, he wouldn't have been so worried and would not have pushed Mahir to make risky decisions.

"Risk isn't about speed, it's about the environment"

Chapter – 22

POWER OF PATIENCE

Ayush, a young man from Bhayander, took the train to Churchgate every day for work. The Mumbai local trains were his routine, noisy but familiar. At Goregaon, his train would always halt for a couple of minutes on the platform. As he waited and looked outside from his window seat, he would always notice the trains departing from Goregaon to Churchgate on the other platform. He felt an inexplicable feeling of urgency every time the other train left before his train. He felt like he was losing those few minutes every day by not switching trains.

One day, as he boarded the train, he decided to act on his impulses and save a few minutes during the stop at Goregaon. As usual, his train reached Goregaon and stopped. He looked outside the window and saw another train waiting on the other platform going towards Churchgate.

Ayush checked his watch— in a moment of impulsive decision-making, Ayush, fuelled by the desire to save time, decided to take a chance. Convinced that his train would wait longer, he made a spontaneous choice. He quickly got off at Goregaon and caught the other train. Ayush was exhilarated. He had shaved off a few minutes from his commute, and the thrill of his impulsive decision lingered.

Having succeeded once, he gained so much confidence that he did this the next day as well. He looked at the other passengers on his train with pity as he was convinced, he was saving more time by switching trains unlike them. However, on the third day, Ayush ran across the station, but just as he stepped onto the platform, he heard a whistle and realised that his original train had left earlier without him. As he disappointedly made his way towards his coach, an announcement crackled over the speakers, "The 10:50 am train from Goregaon to Churchgate will be slightly delayed. We apologise for any inconvenience caused." Panic set in. Ayush realised his impulsive decision had backfired. The train he meant to catch was running late, and the one he left was already gone.

If you were in Ayush's place, would you have had the tenacity to wait patiently on the train? What does this teach you about the probability of actions?

Points to Ponder:

132. Action bias, the belief that wealth creation requires constant movement and decision-making, often pressurises investors to constantly make changes. We succumb to the notion that if we aren't actively doing something, we're falling behind. This

mindset, fuelled by guilt and the fear of missing out, is a breeding ground for poor decisions.

133. The media plays a pivotal role in this narrative. Headlines, articles, and expert opinions are crafted to trigger a call to action. The guilt we feel for not being in perpetual motion becomes the leverage they exploit to keep us engaged in the market, often to our detriment. Hence, we must learn to ignore the news.

134. Ayush had hoped to save time but then was stuck waiting for the delayed train. He realised that trying to outsmart the system had only made him waste more time. Similarly, more action does not necessarily translate to more wealth. The incessant need to act can hinder wealth creation. The key is to discern when to take action and when to resist the influence of external factors.

135. The history of the Sensex, which started at a humble 100 points in 1979 and eventually climbed to around 74000 in 2024, serves as a poignant example. Despite its impressive growth many individual investors did not experience proportionate success in the Sensex. The reason lies in the compulsion to constantly tinker with investments. Investors who resist the temptation to intervene and allow their investments to weather the storms often reap greater rewards.

136. Think of it as choosing between a direct train and a train with connecting changes. The direct train will take you safely to your destination even if it is a little slow. But in the case of connecting changes, even a slight delay between changing trains might make you miss your second train altogether.

137. Amidst all the little actions that you make, you might make one right action which will lead you to believe that it happened because of your skill. You then become overconfident. But the truth is that one action with a positive outcome is a fluke.

138. Data analysis revealed that individuals who invested in the equity market three decades ago and subsequently passed away yielded higher returns than those who actively managed their portfolios during that period. The funds, left untouched, continued to grow. This underscores the power of inaction in wealth accumulation. Being 'dead' in terms of taking action can ironically lead to more financial gains.

139. When investing for the long term to multiply wealth, minor price fluctuations shouldn't be a concern. Whether you buy at 5-10% higher or lower won't significantly impact your returns in the long run. Many people avoid automated investment plans like SIPs (Systematic Investment Plans), believing they need to time the market perfectly. However, they often waste time waiting for the "right" moment. In reality, whether you

invest at ₹90, ₹100, or ₹110 will have little effect on your returns over 10 or 20 years. These small differences are insignificant when it comes to long-term investments. What is important is that you sit on the train before it leaves the station.

140. Every action in the financial realm comes at a cost. Even if we do book profits, we will always be in a hurry to re-invest and might end up investing in the wrong product at the wrong time. This is what we call reinvestment risk.

141. Action can be exciting, but excitement is expensive. Investing is boring, but being boring will make you money.

"Not every action requires a reaction."

Chapter – 23

BLOOMING AMIDST STORMS

In the lovely town of Nainital, lived Namita, a woman with a small dream—to create a tiny homely garden in her backyard. Excited, she visited the local nursery in March, the peak of spring. The vibrant colours of the flowers there mesmerised her, and she couldn't resist bringing home a bunch of hibiscus and marigolds.

Namita planted the flowers with so much hope and care. For a whole month, her garden looked like a beautiful painting. But then, one by one, the flowers started to wilt and die. She tried her best, watering and looking after them, but the flowers just wouldn't come back.

By October, things got even sadder. The leaves on her plants started falling, and her once lively garden turned into bare sticks. Heartbroken, Namita went back to the nursery owner, afraid that she had somehow hurt her plants.

With a compassionate smile, the nursery owner assured Namita that she hadn't done anything wrong. Most plants bloom according to their seasons. Marigolds and hibiscus, she explained, were spring plants that naturally rested during autumn. Namita's garden was merely going through its seasonal cycle. The key was patience. Namita heaved a sigh of relief, she decided to trust the seasons and wait.

But what about her garden? She couldn't just let it look unkempt and depressing. The nursery owner, seeing Namita's disappointment, suggested adding different plants to her garden. Plants like hydrangeas could bloom in the summer, and evergreen ones would stay green all year.

What can Namita's garden teach us about dealing with volatility? How does adding different plants to Namita's garden help with preparing for seasonal uncertainties?

Points to Ponder:

142. Do not make investment decisions based purely on historical returns. Namita bought the hibiscuses and marigolds because she saw that they were in bloom. But soon after she planted them, the flowers withered. Similarly, there is no guarantee that just because an investment has provided good returns in the past, it will do so in the future as well.

143. Namita monitored her flowers every day, and even a single leaf falling became a source of stress. Had she monitored them during their blooming season, she would have realised that her plants were very healthy. Investing in equity can be a bit like that

as well. It is like riding a roller coaster and this volatility can be unsettling.

144. We tend to see instruments like real estate and gold as safe investment options simply because we cannot and do not monitor their value every single day. But with equity, we see the value of our investments change every day. Now, it is natural to feel nervous but to achieve significant growth in investments, one needs to learn to be comfortable with volatility. And to do that, the first step is to stop monitoring our investments daily.

145. Time is a crucial factor in dealing with market fluctuations. If you only look at the daily ups and downs, it might seem scary. But if you zoom out and look at how things have changed over many years, you can look at the bigger picture. For example, the NIFTY index jumps around a lot each day, but over a decade, you will notice that overall, it has only gone up. This is why it's crucial to focus on your long-term investments. So, if you have enough time in hand to let your investments mature, then the daily volatility should not be a factor.

146. Diversification means not putting all your eggs in one basket. Just like the nursery owner advised Namita to plant a variety of flowers, if you spread your money across different types of investments, in different asset classes like equity, gold, real estate, debt etc, it helps reduce the volatility. Even

within asset classes, you can further diversify. For instance, your equity can be spread across different market caps and sectors. So, even if one part of your investment isn't doing well, the others might be doing better, balancing things out and lowering your stress.

147. Ultimately, if you want to make significant growth in your investments, you must learn how to be friends with volatility. You need to learn to be comfortable with the ups and downs of the market. Volatility exists everywhere. Vendors and businessmen, especially those selling seasonal items, capitalise on peak seasons when demand is high and make up for slower periods when sales may be scarce. Successful businessmen don't shy away from volatility—they leverage it to their advantage.

"Volatility itself isn't risky; the real risk is misunderstanding it."

Chapter – 24

NO PIT-STOPS

The Patel family eagerly packed their car, gearing up for an adventure-filled road trip. Mr. and Mrs. Patel, along with their lively 11-year-old daughter Riya and their playful 5-year-old son Dhairya, were thrilled about their journey from Bengaluru to Ooty. They planned to depart at 6:00 AM, anticipating a four-hour drive to reach their destination.

As they cruised along the highway, laughter filled the car, punctuated by Dhairya 's occasional outbursts of excitement. Halfway into their journey, they reached a bustling food court nestled amidst the hills. It was the perfect spot for a pit stop—a chance to refuel both their bodies and their car.

After a hearty breakfast and a quick restroom break, the Patels were ready to hit the road again. However, Dhairya was adamant that he didn't need to use the restroom. "We have a long way to go after this, there won't be any other stops afterwards," Mr. Patel warned Dhairya. "No, I'll be fine, I promise!" Dhairya exclaimed.

They continued their journey amidst the curvy roads when Mrs. Patel noticed that Dhairya was too quiet. She turned around to check up on him. His face was contorted and she instantly realised what was happening. "You need to pee, don't you?" she sighed at Dhairya. He sheepishly nodded. "Can you hold it?" Mr. Patel asked him. "I can't, I have to go!" he whined. It was too dangerous for them to stop their car on the winding roads. Mr. Patel desperately scanned their surroundings for a solution.

Spotting a small *dhaba* nestled at the side of the road, he quickly veered off the highway. The family rushed inside, grateful for the timely respite. Dhairya, relieved, emerged from the restroom with a triumphant grin. Dhairya's restroom break put them half an hour behind schedule.

As they drove, Mrs. Patel suddenly spotted a vendor selling fresh sugarcane juice on the side of the road. Excited by the prospect of a refreshing treat, she urged her husband to make a brief stop. Succumbing to the temptation, they stopped, savouring the moment amidst the scenic beauty. However, this impromptu detour further delayed their arrival. As they ascended the winding roads of the ghats, Riya began to feel queasy from the constant curves. The motion sickness took its toll, and they had to pull over so she could empty her stomach. Mr. Patel quickly bought a bottle of water from a nearby roadside stall to help ease her discomfort.

The extra stops put them behind schedule. The journey that was supposed to take them four hours took six instead and they were late for their check-in at their hotel in Ooty. Nevertheless, they enjoyed whatever remaining time they had left and had a memorable holiday.

Could the Patels have avoided the delay? How could they have planned for the trip better?

Points to Ponder:

148. When you invest for any goal, your investment period should be divided into two distinct phases: accumulation and distribution. The accumulation phase suggests the time frame in which you focus on accumulating and building wealth for your goal. This typically spans from around age 22 to 60, when you are actively earning.

149. Distribution is the time frame in which you utilise the wealth that you have amassed in the accumulation phase. This is when your goal has arrived and it is time for you to spend on it. It can be a short, specific moment like buying a car, or can even be as long as twenty years when it comes to bigger goals like buying a house, children's education and retirement.

150. The challenge arises when these phases become blurred. During the accumulation phase, focus only on investing and don't pull out from your investments. If you know that you are going to need that extra money in the short term then don't invest it in the first place, invest a lower amount instead. Had Dhairya also used the washroom at the food court like the family had planned, they wouldn't have to take extra stops along the way.

This led them to be late for their check-in. Similarly, the more stops you take during your accumulation phase, the longer it's going to take to reach your goal.

151. On the other hand, during the distribution phase, focus only on pulling out the money required from those specific investments and do not reinvest the money until your goal has been fully achieved. You cannot get carried away with returns during the distribution phase.

152. Not sticking to the accumulation and distribution phase leads to unnecessarily pulling out and re-investing in the middle of an investment which also comes with its own set of risks, be it the additional taxes that you have to pay, the management cost or the reinvestment risk that comes with it. If you don't get the right moment to then reinvest that money, you will end up creating a greater potential loss for yourself. We don't want to compromise on our goals nor do we want to compromise on our returns.

153. Treat each financial goal as a separate entity, requiring its dedicated investment strategy. If you have separate financial plans for your different goals—retirement, buying a house, children's education and expenses, you will not have to prematurely withdraw from any of your funds and you can make adjustments to one goal, without affecting the others. You need to adapt to the tree

systems and plan for all your different goals right from the beginning. Let all the different branches work in parallel. This way you have a longer time to achieve all your goals.

154. When choosing an investment product, make sure that its timelines match your accumulation and distribution phase. The fastest and easiest way to get to a destination is a non-stop drive and that's what you should be looking for in your investment products as well.

155. It is also important to maintain a buffer or emergency corpus with at least six to nine months of your living expenses as well as EMI instalments. This layer of financial safety ensures that you won't need to derail your plans midway due to unforeseen circumstances.

"Accumulate without distraction, distribute without hesitation."

Chapter – 25

THE POWER OF LETTING GO

Amit, Mita, and their son, Advait—decided to treat themselves to a casual dinner out. It was a rare occasion for the busy trio to spend quality time together, and they settled on a cosy fast-food joint nearby.

As they approached the counter, Amit was about to order their usual combo of burgers and regular fries for Advait when something caught the young boy's eye.

"Look, Papa! Those fries!" Advait pointed excitedly to the neighbouring table where a family was relishing a serving of peri peri fries. The customer added the fries and peri mix to a bag and shook the bag, which intrigued him. Advait's eyes sparkled with curiosity.

"Advait, beta," Mita began, concern etched in her voice, "those might be too spicy for you. Let's stick with regular fries, okay?"

But Advait was adamant. "I want to try them, Mama! They look so yummy!"

With a sigh, Mita exchanged a worried glance with Amit and asked, "Will you be able to finish it all?" "Yes, I promise!" he assured her excitedly. They reluctantly agreed to Advait's request.

Once seated, Advait eagerly pulled out the peri peri fries, shaking the bag with a huge smile. But as soon as he tasted a fry, the fiery spices hit his tongue. Tears welled up in his eyes as he struggled to mask the discomfort.

"Is it too spicy, Advait?" Amit asked gently, "We did warn you, beta."

But Advait, determined not to admit defeat, shook his head stubbornly and continued to munch on the fries, alternating between bites and hurried sips of his milkshake.

Watching their son's valiant effort, Mita and Amit exchanged a knowing glance. It was clear that Advait found the fries spicy, but his innocence and determination were undeniably endearing.

Finally, unable to bear seeing their son in distress any longer, Amit offered to swap his regular fries for Advait's peri-peri ones. With a grateful smile, Advait accepted the gesture, and the family resumed their meal, laughter and love filling the air.

What lesson do you think Advait learned from this? Would he have not suffered less if had just admitted that he was wrong and couldn't tolerate the spiciness?

Points to Ponder:

156. It's human nature to avoid admitting fault. When we invest in a stock, a property, or any other asset,

we tie our self-worth to its success, and admitting that we were wrong feels like a blow to our ego. If Advait had stuck his ground and eaten all the fries, he could have ended up with a burning stomach and ended up vomiting. Similarly, holding on to a bad investment, won't magically turn it into a good one. More often than not, this reluctance to let go only leads to further losses and missed opportunities.

157. We don't book our losses because no one likes to see the red in their portfolio. We become so fixated on the current loss we have made that we forget to calculate the potential loss we can make in the future if we keep holding on to the asset. We make decisions based on the past and ignore the future. The loss has already been made. What we now need to evaluate is if we are going to make more losses in the future. That should be the deciding factor.

158. The key to cutting losses is to shift our mindset from dwelling on past decisions to focusing on future opportunities. Instead of lamenting over sunk costs, we should be looking at the potential for growth elsewhere. Whether it's reallocating funds to a more promising investment or simply cutting our losses and moving on, taking decisive action is essential.

159. Take the example of insurance. Most people have invested in the wrong insurance policy, say equity, real estate or insurance at least once in

their lifetime. But they don't exit it because of the loss and holding the policy till maturity assures a fixed return. But you also need to evaluate the opportunity loss you will be incurring while holding. If better opportunities arise elsewhere, clinging to the history of our investment will only hold us back. This principle also applies to all other asset classes. The key is not to dwell on the mistake but to learn from it and move forward. We need to evaluate our exit cost and opportunity cost side by side to see which one is better for us.

160. When we finally muster the courage to cut our losses, we create space for new opportunities to emerge. We free up resources, both financial and mental, that can be better deployed elsewhere. We regain control of our financial destiny instead of being held captive by past mistakes.

"Cut your losses today before they multiply tomorrow."

Chapter – 26

RISE OR DIE

On a radiant afternoon at Greenfield Elementary, the school sports day was in full swing. Twelve-year-old Naitik stood at the starting line for the race, his heart beating with a mix of excitement and determination. The cheers from the stands filled the air, and among the proud spectators were Naitik's parents, waving enthusiastically and sporting matching supportive smiles.

As the race announcer called for the participants to take their positions, Naitik stood shoulder to shoulder with his classmates, eyes fixed on the finish line. He was determined to win this race, and the support from his parents fuelled his determination.

"Ready, set, clap!" echoed through the sports field, and the runners shot forward like arrows from a bow. Naitik sprinted with all his might, his legs carrying him swiftly down the track. He and a fellow competitor were neck-to-neck for first place, the thrill of the race coursing through his veins.

But then, in a cruel twist of fate, disaster struck. Naitik felt a sudden tug at his foot, and to his horror, he realised his shoelaces had come undone. In an instant, he tripped and tumbled to the ground, watching in despair as his classmates surged ahead.

The cheers from the sidelines, however, didn't falter. His friends shouted words of encouragement, and his parents cheered on him to get back up and run faster to finish the race. In that critical moment, Naitik found a reserve of strength within himself. He sprang to his feet, kicked off his shoes, and sprinted.

The wind rushed past his face as Naitik raced to catch up. With each stride, he closed the gap between himself and his classmates. Although he didn't reclaim the lead, he was able to finish with an impressive time that secured his qualification for the semi-finals.

As Naitik caught his breath in the finish area, his parents rushed to him, beaming with pride and showering him with praise.

Standing in line for the semi-finals, Naitik knew he couldn't afford a repeat of the shoelace incident. With unwavering focus, he meticulously tied his laces super tight, double and triple checking to ensure they were secure. He was determined not to make the same mistake twice, and as the announcer called for the next race, Naitik took his place on the track, ready to show the world the true meaning of resilience and determination.

What options do you think Naitik had when he fell? What do you think is the probability of him falling again?

Points to Ponder:

161. Loss is an inevitable part of the financial journey—a hurdle that tests the resilience of any investor. If you want to achieve your goals in the race of life, you cannot see these setbacks as a permanent defeat. When Naitik fell down, he had three choices.

     - Give up and quit the race.

     - Walk for the rest of the race

     - Run faster and try to win the race

162. Similarly, when investing, the knee-jerk reaction is to cut losses and exit. However, this impulsive move can lead to missed opportunities and potentially worsen the situation. Instead, facing the fall head-on is crucial. Acknowledge the loss, analyse the factors contributing to it, and learn from the experience. Loss is not a signal to abandon the market but a call to reassess and adapt.

163. If Naitik had chosen to walk to the finish line out of fear of falling again, he would have finished the race without falling. But it would only be after the event was over and his efforts would be pointless. People usually switch to safer investments after facing losses. Fixed-income options offer stability, but they don't have enough growth potential to help you win. Ultimately, you aim to achieve your financial goals.

164. When COVID-19 hit, the economy took a hit too, and many investors panicked and left, losing

money. But if you look at how things bounced back later, it shows that running faster pays off. History shows that markets tend to recover from tough times. Just like Naitik now double and triple checks his shoelaces before a race, you need to learn from your mistakes.

165. You can afford to walk only when you have already won the race. Once you've achieved your financial goals, you can focus on protecting your wealth. However, if your goals remain unmet, wealth creation must be your priority. Just like Naitik continued to push forward until the finish line, you need to actively pursue investment and growth strategies to ensure your financial aspirations are fully realised. Balancing wealth protection and wealth creation is key to financial success.

166. When you choose to quit after a setback, you are choosing to quit from your goals. You will never be able to make up your losses by moving to a conservative asset. Just like Naitik, you need to get up and run again. Stay persistent and patient because the market will always recover at some point, which is when you will not only make up for the losses you have incurred but also get your returns. Giving up before you have achieved your goals will always leave you with regrets.

"Run faster after you fall."

Chapter – 27

EXIT BEFORE IT IS TOO LATE

As the sun dipped low on the horizon, casting long shadows across the highway, Aadar felt a surge of excitement. He was on the road from Delhi to Agra, a journey he'd made countless times before. But every time he approached Agra, the anticipation of seeing the Taj Mahal filled him with a renewed sense of wonder.

Driving down the highway, Aadar kept an eye out for the familiar sign signalling the exit for Agra. Finally, it appeared on the horizon, and Aadar's foot pressed down on the accelerator instinctively, eager to reach his destination as soon as possible.

But in his haste, Aadar failed to notice the subtle curve of the road, and before he knew it, he had driven past the exit. Cursing under his breath, he realised his mistake. He glanced at the rearview mirror, seeing the sign fading into the distance. He had missed his chance.

Taking a deep breath to calm his racing heart, Aadar made a quick decision. He would take the next exit and loop back around. It would delay his arrival, but he wasn't about to let it ruin his mood.

As he approached the next exit, Aadar made sure to take the service road well in advance. The service road stretched out before him, flanked by fields on either side. The pace was slower here, but Aadar didn't mind.

Finally, the exit for Agra came into view once again. Spotting the next exit, Aadar made sure to slow down well in advance. He flicked on his turn signal, checked his mirrors, and smoothly took the exit.

What mistake did Aadar make the first time around? How could he have ensured that he reached his destination on time?

Points to Ponder:

167. During long trips, you pay attention to upcoming exits. You ease off the gas pedal, refrain from aggressive manoeuvres, and prepare to exit safely. The same thought process must apply to investments. Just like slowing down on the highway as you near an exit loses a bit of time but is crucial for a safe and timely exit, it is crucial to gradually pull out money from your investments when nearing the exit, Instead of getting greedy, you must slow down and pull out money at least six months to a year before we need the money.

168. One common mistake investors make is they get greedy and wait for the "perfect" time or price to exit their investments. They may need the money, yet they hold on, hoping for even better returns. This behaviour bias can be detrimental. Waiting

too long can result in missing the optimal exit point, leading to lower returns or even losses. Be disciplined in sticking to your plan, even if it means sacrificing some short-term gains. Remember, the goal isn't just to keep driving; it's to reach your destination.

169. Most people don't have an exit plan. Make an exit plan along with your investing plan. Systematic withdrawals are the best way to exit markets.

"Battles aren't won until you are back home safe."

Chapter – 28

THE RIGHT MIX

Vikas had always considered himself to be health-conscious. He hit the gym regularly, sweated it out during intense workouts, and meticulously watched what he ate. However, a routine health check-up revealed a startling truth—he had certain nutrient deficiencies on the lower side.

Perplexed and slightly concerned, Vikas consulted his doctor who suggested he incorporate supplements into his routine. However, the doctor also recommended a visit to a dietician for a more comprehensive understanding of his dietary needs.

Curious and eager to rectify his deficiencies, Vikas made an appointment with the dietician. As he sat across from her in the consultation room, she delved into the fundamentals of a balanced diet.

"Your body requires a variety of nutrients to function optimally," the dietician explained. "This includes carbohydrates, proteins, fruits, vegetables, fibre, and even fats."

Vikas nodded, but a hint of scepticism lingered. "I've been focusing mainly on protein because of my workouts.

I thought cutting out carbs and fats was the way to go for a healthy diet," he admitted.

The dietician smiled gently. "While protein is important for muscle repair and growth, neglecting other nutrients can have adverse effects on your overall health. Carbohydrates provide the energy your body needs to function efficiently, while fats are essential for various bodily functions and the absorption of certain vitamins."

Vikas listened intently as the dietician outlined a plan tailored to his dietary habits and lifestyle. She emphasised the importance of balance and moderation, encouraging him to include a diverse range of foods in his daily meals.

"Think of your meals as a puzzle," she explained. "Each piece represents a different nutrient, and when you put them together correctly, you create a picture of optimal health." The dietician gave him a plan based on his lifestyle and eating habits and made sure to include more foods like oranges that were rich in Vitamin C and nuts that were rich in iron because his reports showed slight deficiency in them.

Over the following weeks, Vikas gradually implemented changes to his eating habits, incorporating a wider variety of foods and paying closer attention to portion sizes.

Do you think Vikas' new approach is better than his earlier one? If yes, why do you think so?

Points to Ponder:

170. To remain healthy, your diet needs diverse types of food. When it comes to your financial portfolio, diversification is an important strategy as well. It spreads out your investments so that even if one part of your portfolio isn't doing well, the others can help balance it out. Under diversification can make your portfolio volatile and risky while over diversification can bring down your rewards.

171. One common challenge in diversification is tunnel vision, where we focus solely on paper assets while overlooking physical assets like real estate or jewellery. This oversight can lead to an imbalanced portfolio. When trying to remain healthy, you need to look at what you eat in an entire day and not just focus on one meal. Similarly, when you assess the total size of your portfolio, considering both paper and physical assets, you will realise how much you have invested in different asset classes. It will show you where you have over-invested and where you have under-invested.

172. Diversification isn't a one-size-fits-all approach. Just like the dietician focused a little more on packing Vikas' diet with Vitamin C and iron-rich foods, the ideal balance varies from person to person, depending on their financial goals, risk tolerance, and current financial standing. For instance, those who have already accumulated enough wealth to cover daily needs and emergencies can explore

high-risk, high-return investment opportunities. You need to align diversification with your unique financial circumstances.

173. People tend to allocate investments equally across different financial assets, assuming it's the safest approach. A common example of this is the way people invest in equity. Let's say someone decides to invest ₹5 lakh in equity, they will invest either ₹50,000 each in 10 different stocks or ₹1 lakh in five mutual funds in the name of diversifying. Even within asset classes, they are equally invested in stocks, mutual funds and fixed deposits. However, the right combination isn't necessarily an equal one.

174. Each asset class plays a unique role in your portfolio's performance, and their weightage should reflect their significance in achieving your objectives. It's about finding the optimal blend that suits your circumstances and aspirations.

175. Just because Vikas liked eating sweets, he could not have more of it. It might make him sick in the long run. Similarly, you cannot invest everything in a particular asset just because it is giving you more rewards. On the other hand, while having too much fat is not good for the body, you require at least some of it in your diet to be able to absorb certain vitamins. Similarly, some investments may underperform compared to others, but their presence contributes to the stability and resilience

of the portfolio over the long haul. Embracing this approach ensures that your investment strategy remains steadfast amid market fluctuations and uncertainties.

176. In mastering portfolio diversification, remember that it's not about chasing the latest trends or aiming for perfection. It's about crafting a well-rounded team of investments that can weather any financial climate and propel you towards your financial goals with confidence.

"True investment wisdom lies in balancing, not equalising."

Chapter – 29

SAFETY FIRST

Samay and his wife, Anjali, decided to check out the new fancy ice cream store that had just opened in their neighbourhood. Known for its customisable options, the shop lets you pick everything—from the number of scoops to the flavours and toppings. They were both excited and didn't want to miss out on the experience.

As they entered the store, the sight of colourful ice cream tubs and an array of toppings dazzled them. Samay loved strawberries, while Anjali preferred chocolate. They were about to place their order when Anjali noticed the toppings counter.

She couldn't resist the tempting variety—sprinkles, brownie chunks, syrup, whipped cream, nuts, and more. But adding toppings would mean that they would also have to pay more. After some discussion, they both decided to share a bowl because the toppings seemed so tempting. They settled on Anjali's choice of chocolate as their base flavour and out of sheer excitement, they ended up adding nearly everything to their bowl.

Finally, they sat down with their creation. The sundae looked magnificent, but as they started eating, they realised that the toppings didn't quite go together. The rich chocolate flavour was drowned out by the syrup's sweetness, while the nuts clashed with the whipped cream.

Before they knew it, they had finished the ice cream too quickly. Despite the indulgence, the small bowl wasn't enough for both of them, leaving them unsatisfied. They ended up spending more on the overloaded sundae than it would have cost to simply order two scoops of their preferred flavours.

Did Samay and Anjali overdo it? Would they have been happier with fewer toppings and more ice cream?

Points to Ponder:

177. Insurance is like ice cream; there are countless options and an overwhelming array of add-ons to choose from. You might get overwhelmed and overindulge in them just like Samay and Anjali did in the ice cream shop. You want to be safe but also not drown yourself in premiums. But how do you make the best choice for you? You need to consider these four crucial factors: risk ownership, risk avoidance, risk minimisation, and risk transfer.

178. Risk ownership refers to the kinds of risks we are prepared to handle ourselves. These are the risks we accept and can pay for ourselves if they materialise. You don't need to take insurance for every minor potential loss, especially if you can bear the consequences and costs associated with these

activities. It's essential to recognise which risks you can manage on your own. Buying insurance for every conceivable risk results in higher premiums and unnecessary expenditure.

179. If you are unable to cover a risk on your own, then you need to consider risk avoidance. This strategy involves steering clear of activities or situations that carry unacceptable levels of risk. If you recognise that you cannot own the risk of a particular action, it's wise to avoid it altogether. For example, if you find that a certain business venture is too volatile and beyond your risk tolerance, avoiding that venture altogether is a prudent choice. By avoiding high-risk situations, you eliminate the potential for certain losses, reducing the necessity for insurance in those areas.

180. However, if you cannot avoid the risk either, then you focus on minimising it. Risk minimisation involves taking steps to reduce the likelihood of a risk event occurring or mitigating its impact. While these actions don't eliminate risks entirely, they significantly reduce the chances of adverse outcomes, thereby lessening the need for extensive insurance coverage.

181. If you cannot avoid the risk or minimise it beyond a point that is comfortable for you to handle on your own, the next step is risk transfer, which is where insurance comes into play. Risk transfer means shifting the financial burden of a potential

loss to an insurance company. This is essential for risks that have a low probability of occurring but would result in significant financial loss if they did. Things like fire insurance, life insurance and health insurance fall into this category. These types of coverage protect you from catastrophic losses that could otherwise be devastating. By transferring such risks to an insurer, you safeguard your financial stability and peace of mind.

182. When deciding on insurance, assess the potential loss that you are protecting yourself from. The probability of that loss occurring should be low, but the potential loss from it should be substantial. Only then do you insure it. Everyday losses, such as minor car repairs or routine medical expenses, can and should be owned and managed personally. However, insuring against events that could lead to severe financial strain, such as major health issues or property damage, is crucial.

183. Just like the toppings simply increased the cost of the ice cream without adding any substantial flavour to it, insurance add-ons are also ways for companies to increase your premium for things that add very little to no value in terms of risk management. Had Samay and Anjali bought two scoops instead of all the different toppings, they would have been more satisfied. Don't get carried away by add-ons, focus on a bigger basic coverage, which is more important. Insurance is meant to protect, not for

the sole purpose of claims. Try 'owning' as many of the add-ons as you can and pay for only those that are necessary. The goal is to secure coverage that shields you from financial setbacks without overpaying for unnecessary features.

"Don't pay for things you don't need."

Chapter – 30

THE MYTH OF ALL-IN-ONE

Lalit was ravenous when he stepped into the burger joint. Craving a chicken burger and a strawberry milkshake, he eagerly approached the counter to place his order. The server, a cheerful young woman, greeted him warmly and began listing the available combos. "You know," she said with a bright smile, "if you get the combo, it's cheaper. You'll get a burger, a drink, fries, and a pudding!"

The idea of saving money tempted Lalit. He opted for the combo, which included a small burger, small fries, a tiny pudding, and a soft drink. However, his heart was set on the strawberry milkshake. The server informed him that the combo only came with soft drinks, but for an additional 100 rupees, he could upgrade to the milkshake. Reluctantly, Lalit decided to stick with the soft drink, thinking he was still getting a good deal.

With his tray full, Lalit returned to his table. As he unwrapped the small burger, he quickly devoured it, but it wasn't enough to satisfy his hunger. The fries, which he hadn't really wanted, only filled him up a little, and the soft drink remained mostly untouched—he just didn't enjoy it. The tiny pudding did little to curb his craving for something sweet. Feeling unsatisfied, Lalit ended up ordering a brownie for dessert, adding to his bill.

As he finished his meal, Lalit realised he was still hungry and had spent more than he intended. If he had just ordered the large burger and the strawberry milkshake like he initially wanted, he would have been satisfied and saved money. Instead, he ended up paying for items he didn't enjoy or need, all because the combo seemed like a good deal at first glance.

Would you choose a combo meal like Ravi's? Have you ever been tempted by a deal, only to regret it later?

Points to Ponder:

184. Life insurance is a lot like a combo meal at a fast-food restaurant. At first glance, the meal deal appears to be a great bargain, offering a variety of items bundled together. However, you might end up with items you don't necessarily need or want. Insurance products often work the same way. They are packaged attractively, combining different benefits into a single policy. While this may seem convenient, it's important to remember that insurance and investment are two distinct needs that should ideally be addressed separately.

185. Insurance is primarily a protective measure, while investment aims to grow your wealth. You will end up with low returns in terms of investment as well

as less coverage in terms of insurance. Just like the combo meal not only ended up increasing Lalit's bill but also left him still hungry, combining the two will only dilute the effectiveness of both.

186. Insurance premiums are big financial commitments. During times of financial stress, you can easily stop your investments, but not paying your insurance premium can give you an additional penalty and you can risk losing your coverage. This will only add to your pre-existing stress. If you separate your insurance from investment and focus only on the coverage you need, your premium can be significantly smaller, making it an easier commitment to follow through.

187. Have you ever had a family member receive their insurance maturity? Has that maturity ever brought some immense joy or even a smile on their face? If you see the inflation-adjusted future value of an insurance maturity you will realise that they don't often justify themselves in long-term policies. This is because we buy insurance based on only numbers without looking at the actual money value. The premium that we pay so painfully in our younger years may value peanuts during maturity when we factor in inflation. The premiums paid in today's value will result in a payout that might be worth less in tomorrow's value due to inflation.

188. Life insurances are meant to safeguard and protect you and your family. The purpose of your life

insurance is to ensure that your family is financially taken care of in the case of your untimely demise. Insurance agents often promote policies with lifelong coverage, which may not be necessary. Once you are financially secure and have fulfilled your responsibilities—such as paying off debts, funding your children's education, their wedding, buying a home and securing your retirement—you may not need life insurance anymore. At this point, maintaining only health insurance is usually sufficient. Life insurance is also only essential for earning members of a family because their income supports the household.

189. Determining how much life insurance coverage you need involves a careful assessment of your financial responsibilities and future obligations. This need-based calculation should account for various factors, including existing debts, ongoing living expenses, education and marriage costs for your children, and retirement planning. For instance, if you have young children, you need sufficient coverage to ensure their education and upbringing in your absence. If you have outstanding loans, the insurance should cover these liabilities to prevent burdening your family.

190. You will generally need a higher amount of insurance coverage in your younger years because you might depend on it for the number of future responsibilities that would still need to be fulfilled.

However, as you grow older, you will need to take care of these responsibilities one by one and bridge this gap with investments. Soon you will realise that you don't need as much protection anymore. So, you can gradually decrease your insurance coverage as you retire.

191. When opting for a combo plan, you typically receive smaller coverage, lower returns, limited investment flexibility, and face liquidity issues. It's advisable to separate the two—purchase the appropriate amount of insurance needed and plan your investments separately.

"Invest wisely, insure thoughtfully, and keep them separate."

Chapter – 31

WHY WHITE WINS

In a tiny locality in Kolkata, the Bajaj's ran a small bakery renowned for its artisanal bread. Every morning, their ovens would fill the air with the rich aroma of freshly baked loaves, drawing customers from miles around. Yet, behind the scenes, the Bajaj's faced a harsh reality.

Each day, the bakery would produce a batch of bread, but not all loaves would make it to the shelves. Some were slightly overbaked, others missed the perfect shape, and a few even became too hard to sell. It was a heartbreaking sight: perfectly good bread wasted, destined to be given away or discarded.

Mr. Bajaj, who meticulously balanced the bakery's books, often pondered the financial strain of this waste. Each loaf discarded was money lost. But he also knew that this unavoidable margin of loss was part of their production process. To achieve that golden crust and fluffy interior that their customers loved, the bakery needed to bake more loaves than they could sell.

If they tried to eliminate waste, they would have to cut corners, compromise on quality, and ultimately lose the essence of what made their bread special. The delicate balance between production and waste was a hidden cost of excellence. It ensured that each loaf met their high standards and, in turn, allowed the bakery to thrive. He just saw it as a cost of production.

Even with that margin of loss, their bakery shone brightly, and their loyal customers kept coming back to taste the true magic of their bread.

Would it be wise for Mr. Bajaj to forgo his profits over minor costs? Have you ever held back from enjoying your finances due to fear of losing some expenses?

Points to Ponder:

192. In a world where financial transactions are increasingly digitised, "cash is king" no longer holds true. However, many people still prefer to keep cash in hand rather than depositing it in the bank, driven by the belief that they are saving money on taxes.

193. This is because you see taxes as money being taken away from you. You are focusing more on the wasted bread rather than the bread that is selling. Instead, be like Mr. Bajaj and just see taxes as a convenience fee or cost for keeping your money safe and perennially usable.

194. The cash approach is not only outdated but also fraught with significant drawbacks. Ideally, the total of what we spend + what we invest + our taxes should be our earnings in our bank account. But our annual expenses exceed our annual earnings

on paper and this gap is widening every year. This is because we are able to earn and spend in cash today. But slowly we will not be able to.

195. The convenience of cash is rapidly diminishing in today's world. With the rise of digital payment methods like UPI and credit cards, using cash for purchases is becoming increasingly difficult. Digital transactions are so convenient that we end up spending via online transactions instead of cash in our daily lives.

196. Bigger expenses like healthcare, your child's education, travel etc. are now becoming impossible to pay for in cash. Cash is losing its utility because of its lack of dependability. What is the point of earning so much money, if you cannot spend it at the most important times? Despite being rich, cash will make you feel inadequate. Your money should help you feel secure.

197. With fewer and fewer places to spend cash, it can only be used for spending on unnecessary luxuries and shopping. Therefore, the more cash you earn, the more you'll be forced to waste it without actually being able to build any financial security. To build wealth and secure your future, investing is essential and you cannot do that without white money.

198. Transitioning to a white money corpus now helps bridge the gap between your financial realities and

future needs. By gradually shifting your financial practices towards legal transactions, you mitigate the risk of future shortfalls and ensure that you are prepared for unforeseen expenses or opportunities.

"Cash used to be king, but today banks hold the power."

Chapter – 32

THE EMOTIONAL REWARD

Naman, his wife Manisha, and their two children were crammed into a single room in the family's large house. Every inch of space was filled with their belongings, and it always seemed as though there wasn't enough air for everyone. In the mornings, the chaos began as soon as the sun rose. Naman would be getting ready for the office, while Manisha hurriedly tried to pack lunches. The children, who had exams coming up, struggled to concentrate on their books amidst the noise. Inevitably, there was a disagreement—a missing tie, a misplaced book, differing opinions on breakfast—and every morning turned into a stressful race against time.

Manisha, who used to be a calm and collected person, now felt frazzled and on edge. She had no privacy, no space of her own. Even when Naman was at work, the house was full of family members constantly seeking her attention. She couldn't find a moment of peace to read a book, enjoy a cup of tea, or even take a nap. At night, after Naman returned home from a long and stressful day at the office, he hoped for a brief escape, a few quiet moments with Manisha, but those were rare. Their shared room, already cramped with the children's schoolwork scattered everywhere, became another battlefield of unmet needs.

What weighed on Naman the most was the constant interference from his extended family. No decision was simple. From how they parented their children to where they went on weekends, everyone had an opinion. The pressure to conform, to keep everyone happy, was suffocating. Even if Naman and Manisha wanted to make small changes to improve their own lives, the family's endless input made everything feel complicated.

Is Naman's financial savings worth the trade-off of living with his parents? Can Naman's own family find happiness in the current living situation?

Points to Ponder:

199. Homeownership is a symbol of pride across the globe. It has existed for generations. Buying a home is an emotional decision, but if your financial situation allows, it is something that should be done. If you look at it logically, the numbers might dictate that renting is more economical, but having your own place to live provides you with stability that is much more important for your psychological needs. Many modern financial theories say otherwise. This is because they are geared towards salaried individuals in developed countries and might not fully consider the unique circumstances of India.

200. For people who are salaried and unsure of when they might have to relocate, home ownership is not

an immediate need. It comes at a later stage in their life. However, for those who are rooted in a specific city and plan to stay there for the long term, home ownership offers stability and a place for relaxation.

201. In India, large joint families are common. People live with elders, siblings, and children all under one roof. While there are some benefits to this living arrangement, privacy and freedom are very limited. And not everyone is open to the idea of building separate houses or living spaces for younger generations.

202. A house is not an investment, it is a necessity. Don't look at it in terms of returns. Even a small home gives you a sense of security, safety, pride respect and belonging in a community. Imagine having to leave for work every day after a stressful morning and having to return to the same stress every night. When you have your own space, you are able to keep your peace of mind.

203. Buying a house when financially comfortable provides a secure haven, especially in your later years. How will you feel about moving houses every two years when you are sixty? It will be such a hassle. Renting and moving houses can be feasible when you are younger, but you can't move houses every two years in your sixties.

204. A lot of people think that investing a large sum of money in their own business instead of buying a

house will allow them to earn more. But prioritise buying a house. The more at peace you are, the more efficient you can be at work. Additionally, because you now have a sense of stability, it increases your risk appetite and opens you up to other opportunities.

205. However, this does not mean that you buy a house without looking at your finances. Plan it, act according to your budget and buy it as early as possible. Don't take on unaffordable loans in order to buy a home. It should not become a burden.

206. Similar to buying a house, car ownership has both financial and emotional aspects. Cars are used assets but they are giving you other things that cannot be monetarily calculated. If you can afford it, then buy it. Owning a car eliminates dependence on cabs, saves time, reduces stress, and offers more comfort for you and your family.

207. If you can afford it then buy the most extravagant house or car you want. But if you can't afford it, then work towards it and prioritise it. Buy a small home and a small car, but buy one.

"Sacrificing happiness is not financial success."

Chapter – 33

CHOOSE YOUR POISON

Rhea sat across from her dietician, staring at the meal plan in her hands. Everything looked reasonable until she saw the replacements for sugar—stevia and jaggery. She raised an eyebrow.

"But aren't these sugars too?" she asked, glancing up.

The dietician smiled knowingly. "Yes, they are. All sugars are bad in excess. But the reality is, we can't completely live without them. We need sweetness in our lives—whether for taste, energy or just to keep sane."

Rhea frowned, trying to process it all. "So… why these? Why not just stick with regular sugar?"

The dietician leaned back in her chair. "It's about choosing your poison. White processed sugar is the worst—it's stripped of nutrients and spikes your blood sugar levels, which leads to crashes, cravings, and, over time, serious health issues. Stevia is plant-based and has zero calories, but it can taste a bit odd. Jaggery is more natural, packed with minerals, and digests slower, but it's still sugar. None of them are perfect, but stevia and jaggery are the lesser evils compared to the highly processed white stuff."

Rhea nodded slowly. She didn't love the idea of giving up her regular sugar, but she couldn't ignore the logic. She had to choose her poison, and if it meant switching to something slightly better, she was willing to try. Small steps, she reminded herself, as she folded the meal plan and tucked it into her bag.

Can we ever fully avoid what's bad for us? Or do we just choose the lesser evil and manage the consequences?

Points to Ponder:

208. Loans are a double-edged sword. They have the power to propel you toward your dreams or pull you down into a financial mess. Borrowing is always a risk, but if you have to borrow then like Rhea you need to pick your poison. You need to learn to differentiate between good loans and bad loans.

209. Good loans help you reach your goals by leveraging your present resources to secure a brighter future. For example, loans taken out for your or your child's education, for upskilling yourself, or business loans. These loans are investments in yourself and your potential. The value of what you buy with a good loan usually increases over time, or it helps you improve your income potential. Other examples of good loans are those that give you a sense of stability. Home loans are necessities for your peace of mind and a healthy life.

210. On the flip side, bad loans are like quicksand—they can pull you under and trap you in a cycle of debt. These loans are typically used for one-time purchases or experiences that do not generate any future income or appreciation in value. They are linked to instant gratification and can lead to long-term financial strain. Car loans, personal loans and credit card debt are some examples of bad loans. Another example of bad loans that is rampant in Indian culture is wedding loans. Taking out huge amounts of loans just for one day to put up a social farce is not beneficial to anyone.

211. It's important to remember that not all debt is bad. Even if you can afford to pay for something outright. Sometimes, taking a loan can be a strategic move, allowing you to maintain liquidity for emergencies or future opportunities. However, this approach requires discipline and careful planning.

212. The key to using debt effectively is to borrow smartly. Before taking out a loan, evaluate your financial situation, net worth, and liquidity. Ask yourself whether the loan will help you build wealth or if it will be a burden on your finances.

213. A lot of people take out loans without planning a proper repayment plan and then end up having to constantly adjust their lives according to these loans. Prioritise paying off bad debt quickly, while managing good debt strategically. Pay off your high-interest loans first.

214. Remember, choose your poison. Loans are bad, but if you have taken one, then take a good one for the right reasons and don't feel guilty about it.

"The right debt can build success; the wrong debt can be a pitfall."

Chapter – 34

MORE IS LESS

Garima was shopping at her local grocery mart. As usual, she pushed her shopping cart through the aisles, filling it with things she needed for her household. As she reached the cereal aisle, she went to pick up her usual fibrous oatmeal cereal, when something caught her eye.

Despite the cereal's popularity, the grocery store's management had devised a plan to boost sales further. She saw packs of two that she had not seen before. And with each pack, you got a complimentary pack of the new chocolate-flavoured cereal.

After a short moment of consideration, Garima decided to purchase the combo with the complimentary chocolate-flavoured cereals instead.

However, a week after her purchase, Garima realised she had made a mistake. While she did love the oatmeal cereal, it was not something she consumed every day. Finishing those two boxes of cereals before their expiry date would be a task. Additionally, upon tasting the chocolate cereal, she quickly realised that although it was tasty, it was too sugary to be a viable breakfast option.

As days turned into weeks, Garima struggled to finish the two boxes of cereals before their expiration date. The chocolate ones, although enjoyed as an occasional treat, remained largely untouched.

Garima couldn't help but feel overwhelmed by the surplus of cereals and the mismatch between her expectations and reality.

Why do you think the supermarket put an offer on an already successfully selling product? Do you think the offer was beneficial to Garima?

Points to Ponder:

215. The supermarket had revised the offer not for the oatmeal cereals that were already doing well, but for the chocolate ones that weren't selling. The offer was designed to clear out excess inventory and maximise profits. While Garima assumed that she was getting a good deal by getting more than what she paid in return, she ended up purchasing and consuming more cereal than she usually would have.

216. When we hear the term 'return' in the context of finance, it often conjures images of growth, prosperity, and success. We're bombarded with advertisements promising high returns on investments, enticing us to jump on board. But let's pause and reconsider: is return truly the key to

our financial well-being, or has it just been cleverly marketed to us?

217. Return is a powerful sales tool used by financial institutions, bankers, and investment firms to lure us into their offerings. The promise of high returns triggers our greed. We've been conditioned to believe that it holds the key to our financial security and success. The word return provokes us to make wrong financial decisions.

218. People are ready to take on even negative returns like debt when faced with monetary needs. If returns were truly our top priority, we would never make choices like buying smartphones on EMI. What we truly desire is the freedom to spend our money without constraints. We may believe that we need high returns to secure our financial future, but in reality, what we need is the assurance that we can access our funds when necessary. Negative returns will never make us unhappy as long as we get to spend that money.

219. We are often drawn to new products that promise high returns in the market. While these can be appealing, it is generally wiser to stick with well-known and proven options. Waiting a few years to see how new products perform before investing can help mitigate risks and ensure more stable returns.

220. The allure of high returns can be enticing. But we mustn't lose sight of the bigger picture. If Garima

had just bought one pack like she always did, she could have enjoyed the cereals more by eating them whenever she felt like it instead of focussing on finishing them. Likewise, growing our money is important, but not at the expense of our ability to enjoy it.

221. Rethink the way you perceive returns. Ultimately, what matters most is not how much our money grows, but how much we can use and achieve with it. So, by all means, grow your money, but never forget the importance of being able to spend it. Do returns really make us happy?

"Returns are a sales tool."

Chapter – 35

FREE IS A GIMMICK

Omar needed a new pair of jeans, so he decided to head to the mall to find the perfect fit. As he walked through the bustling corridors, his eyes were drawn to a store with bold, red signs advertising sales and offers. Intrigued, he made his way inside, hoping to find a good deal on jeans.

After browsing through racks of denim, Omar finally found a pair that caught his eye. They were just what he was looking for—stylish, comfortable, and priced at ₹4299. Without hesitation, he tried them on and knew they were the ones.

As he approached the checkout counter to make his purchase, the cashier greeted him with a smile. "Sir, we have a special offer today," she said eagerly. "If you spend just ₹800 more, you'll qualify for a free cap worth ₹599."

Omar's interest was piqued at the mention of 'free', even though he didn't particularly need a new cap. He glanced around the store, searching for something else to buy to reach the ₹5000 threshold.

However, everything seemed to be either too expensive or not quite what he was looking for. Just as he was about to give up, his eyes landed on a display of graphic tees. Among them was one with a design he thought was wearable, priced at ₹2799. Omar grabbed the shirt and added it to his purchase.

As he walked out of the store with his new jeans, free cap, and stylish tee in hand, Omar couldn't help but feel a sense of satisfaction. He had managed to score a great deal on his purchase and walked away with more than he had originally planned. With a smile on his face, he headed home, eager to show off his new additions to his wardrobe.

Do you think Omar really got a great deal at the end of the day? Was the cap he got actually free?

Points to Ponder:

222. Although Omar was fully satisfied with his purchase, it would have been a lot cheaper for him to just buy the cap instead. What would have been even cheaper was to have remembered that he did not need or want the cap in the first place.

223. The word "free" holds a very powerful sway over our consumer psychology. Marketers understand that when something is offered at no cost, we as consumers, perceive its value to be higher than it actually is. This is known as the 'zero price effect', which, like Omar, leads us to buy items or services we may not need simply because we think they

come at no apparent cost. The truth, however, is that the idea of 'free' is a gimmick.

224. Nothing in this world truly comes for free; everything has an objective. If you are given free samples of a product, it is to make you use a product you never would have otherwise and make you buy it the next time. If you get a free ticket to a concert; the ticket might be free but will you not end up spending thousands and thousands of rupees at the concert venue on food and drinks? You might even spend more than you usually would, simply because you got the ticket for free.

225. We carry forward this same behaviour with our finances as well. This is why we get attracted to investment schemes that come with the word 'tax-free'. The best example would be financial products that fall under Section 80 C. The government gives you a tax reduction of ₹1.5 lakh if you invest a certain amount in the products listed under this section. Because you don't want to let go of the tax concession you end up investing in these products, regardless of how low their returns are and whether they align with your goals or not. The same goes with insurances that offer you tax-free maturity, PPF, the Sukanya Samriddhi scheme etc. Just because something is free, doesn't mean that it is inherently good for you. You can make more money if you just pay the tax and invest the money elsewhere.

226. Paying tax can be a wiser move if it is ultimately giving us a higher profit. We must also look at other aspects like liquidity. Is avoiding tax worth blocking ourselves from being able to use the funds as and when we need it? The price of free is liquidity and opportunity for higher reward. The next time you encounter the word 'free', pause and consider the true cost behind the illusion. Be it during spending or investing, resisting impulsive thoughts can help you make better financial choices.

"Nothing in life is truly free, everything comes at a price."

Chapter – 36

RISKY REELS

Siddharth, a mid-twenties IT professional in Mumbai, found himself a seat in the crowded local train on his way back home. As he scrolled through Instagram to pass his time, he stumbled upon posts that depicted a world far removed from his daily grind. Images of luxurious lifestyles, exotic destinations, and the latest tech gadgets flooded his screen. He found himself entangled in the allure of social media trends. While scrolling through his feeds, he stumbled upon posts glorifying cryptocurrency investments, promising quick wealth and financial freedom.

As Siddharth delved deeper into the world of cryptocurrency, he came across a webinar hosted by a charismatic financial expert who claimed to have mastered the art of crypto investments. Intrigued by the promise of exclusive insights and strategies for financial success, Siddharth signed up without a second thought.

The webinar proved to be a persuasive experience. The expert spoke eloquently about the transformative power of cryptocurrencies and how they could pave the way for unprecedented wealth. The success stories shared during the session fuelled Siddharth's belief that he had found the key to financial freedom.

Eager to test the waters, Siddharth began with a modest investment of a couple of thousand rupees. To his surprise, the initial returns were impressive. The thrill of making quick profits fuelled his confidence, and he gradually increased the stakes, putting a substantial portion of his savings into various cryptocurrencies.

In the following weeks, Siddharth anxiously monitored his investments. The volatile digital market, much like the fast-paced nature of his IT job, began taking a toll on him. The very social media platforms that once inspired him now added to his worries as he witnessed the values of his digital assets fluctuating wildly.

Amidst the chaos, a sudden drop in prices shook Siddharth to the core. Overnight, a significant part of his savings disappeared, leaving him in a state of panic. Envy of the seemingly successful lives portrayed by influencers and crypto experts turned into regret as Siddharth grappled with the consequences of his impulsive decisions.

After losing a chunk of his savings, Siddharth realised he needed to learn more about finance and cryptocurrency. He asked experienced investors for advice and dove into educational resources. Shifting from envy to understanding, he decided to decode the complexities of digital currencies, and if they were actually worth it by hiring professionals instead of learning from the same free influencers who first caught his eye.

What lessons can Siddharth's journey teach us about managing money? How does Siddharth's experience highlight the need for accurate financial knowledge?

Points to Ponder:

227. Today, the internet is like a gigantic library filled with all sorts of financial information. Social media, in particular, is a mixed bag. While it's great for connecting with other investors, it can also throw a lot of confusing and sometimes wrong advice our way. The challenge today is finding the right information for you. It's like picking the right pair of shoes in a store with a thousand options. You need to choose the ones that fit—in this case, the information that matches your financial goals and situation.

228. Not everyone advising on social media cares about helping you. Some folks just want to look good or make money. High follower counts do not necessarily equate to expertise; popularity doesn't guarantee sound financial counsel. Most influencers only care about views, likes, follows or sponsored content that can be monetizable. It's important to be smart and use your own judgement.

229. Social media can also mess with our heads and make us feel like we're missing out on something big. This is what happened with Siddharth as well. There is no one right way to get rich overnight.

If someone is promising, you need to use your rationality. The fear of missing out can push us to make quick decisions that are detrimental to our financial health. To avoid this, we need to filter out all the extra noise online and stick to a plan that makes sense for us.

230. Moreover, social media algorithms only present you with information that you want to or like to see. Posts that are presented to you are not always chronological. This might result in you relying on obsolete or paid articles. Your feed may be filled with outdated research reports on stocks or funds. Even numbers that are presented as facts can be manipulated to present even losing investments as attractive, leading to potentially harmful decisions.

"Social media can mislead—select with care and choose what truly fits you."

Chapter – 37

THE DIY EFFECT

Shanoy had been running his own online sneaker business. He realised that he needed a strong social media presence in order to attract more customers, especially the younger generation who was more into buying and collecting sneakers.

After interviewing several social media managers and digital marketers, he decided it wasn't worth paying someone just to post on social media on his behalf. He decided to take on the task of managing his social media marketing himself. He had seen numerous tutorials and guides online, convincing him that handling it solo would be a breeze.

However, reality soon set in. The demands of his business piled up, leaving him with little time to dedicate to social media. Despite his initial enthusiasm, Shanoy found himself struggling to keep up with the regularity and quality of posts required to maintain a strong online presence. Juggling between managing his business operations and trying to stay on top of the latest trends in digital marketing proved to be overwhelming.

As days turned into weeks, Shanoy realised that his DIY approach to social media marketing was not yielding the desired results. He often found himself falling behind schedule, unable to engage with his audience effectively or adapt to the rapidly changing landscape of online platforms.

It was taking up too much of his time and effort as a result of which it was affecting his main business operation as well. Other aspects of his business that demanded his attention. Shanoy needed to find a way to sustain all his business roles.

Do you think DIY was the more economical decision to make? Would the self-managed social media handle be a better decision in the long run?

Points to Ponder:

231. Because of the infinite supply of information available to us online, people are getting more and more drawn to the DIY (Do It Yourself) culture. From fixing household appliances to self-diagnosing medical conditions and even managing finances, the internet will make us believe that we can do it all. Who doesn't want to learn a new skill? It helps utilise your free time.

232. Shanoy ended up spending time on his social media that he could have otherwise spent on expanding his business. Had he paid a skilled marketer to do the job, things would have turned out differently. The same goes for hiring financial advisors or professionals. Many of us, like Shanoy's little DIY

project, believe it is unnecessary to hire experts and that we can handle our finances on our own. The root mentality behind this is that we resent the idea of someone else earning from our money. We don't like parting with our hard-earned money, especially when we think there is a cheaper alternative.

233. The DIY mentality fails to acknowledge the expertise and experience that professionals bring to the table. While it is tempting to believe we can learn to do everything ourselves, there is no way a two-hour webinar or fifteen-day course can teach you as much as someone with 15 years of experience in the same industry.

234. Even if you do have the expertise, your time is very important. Even after his long hours at work Shanoy, instead of resting, had to pour more sweat into building a social media presence. Instead of wasting your time and resources, you could use the time spent learning and executing financial strategies to enhance your industry skills and focus on growing your primary income instead. Upgrading yourself in your own profession can yield better monetary rewards.

235. Another aspect is the consistency. Even after all his efforts, Shanoy found himself falling behind on his social media schedules due to the myriad of other responsibilities on his shoulders. He could have easily hired a manager who would have spent all his time studying and strategising, making it more

effective. Similarly, the key to healthy finances is consistency and it can be quite challenging to attain the discipline required to maintain that consistency.

236. Finally, the absolute main reason the DIY approach fails, especially in finance, is that it overlooks the emotional behaviours of decision-making. Just like doctors would not want to operate on family and lawyers refrain from representing themselves in court, managing one's finances can be clouded by personal biases and attachments. A professional advisor can offer more objective guidance.

237. Investing online seems easier but the actual challenge lies in the support that is required afterwards. Calling & waiting in long customer care queues can be daunting, especially when you don't know who is on the other end. A lot of people face challenges with assimilating old documents and keeping up with the changing guidelines.

238. DIY can still be a viable option in the initial days when your corpus is small, and you have fewer responsibilities. But as you grow up and begin earning more, it becomes difficult to spare the time to manage your finances. The corpus becomes huge and expert guidance becomes necessary to navigate it. If you are still inclined towards a more hands-on approach with your finances, then opt for managed portfolios, like mutual funds, that allow you to make investment decisions but under the expertise

of professional fund managers. If you do choose to expose yourself to stocks, then restrict yourself to a few stocks to make it easy for you to research and keep track of.

239. The whole idea is not to save on the management fee but to earn more rewards on our investments. Professionals take a fee but give you an additional edge. Saving on their fees will save you less as compared to the rewards generated by an expert.

"DIY saves money, but experts help you earn more."

Chapter – 38

THE BLAME GAME.

Rohit's son Aryan just turned 18 and had been pestering his father to teach him how to drive. Finally giving in, Rohit patiently guided his son through the intricacies of driving. As Aryan gradually gained confidence, Rohit decided it was time for the next challenge—navigating the infamous Chennai traffic.

On a busy afternoon, they found themselves at a congested junction, waiting for the signal to grant them passage. Aryan, behind the wheel, was calm and composed. His hands gripped the steering wheel with determination, his eyes scanning the surroundings. It was a test of skill and nerves for every Chennai driver daily.

When the signal finally shifted from red to green, Aryan cautiously accelerated. But in the blink of an eye, a rickshaw, driven by a hurried driver, recklessly zoomed past them, violating the signal. Aryan's reflexes kicked in, and he slammed the brakes, narrowly avoiding a collision. However, the car behind them wasn't as fortunate and collided with their bumper.

As the father and son stepped out of the car, relief washed over them as they observed the minimal damage to the car behind. Their own vehicle, however, bore the brunt of the impact with a noticeable dent on the bumper.

Rohit, though visibly frustrated, maintained his composure. "Aryan, this is a lesson," he said, gesturing towards the damaged bumper. "You did well to brake on time, but you should have been more cautious. In this city, you'll encounter drivers like that *rickshawwala* every day."

Aryan protested, "But Dad, he broke the signal! It's not our fault."

Rohit, placing a hand on Aryan's shoulder, explained, "It doesn't matter whose mistake it was. What matters is the outcome and who it affects. We have to take responsibility for our safety on the road. Chennai is full of unpredictable drivers, and it's our duty to navigate through that chaos without getting harmed."

Whose fault do you think it was? Was Rohit right in scolding Aryan?

Points to Ponder:

240. Rohit taught Aryan an important lesson—when it comes to our safety, we are responsible for it, regardless of who is at fault. The same goes for our financial decisions. It doesn't matter who you entrusted with your money or who made the wrong call. It is ultimately your money and hence, your loss to bear.

241. This is why choosing who to invest with is a decision that needs to be made very carefully.

When it comes to spending our money, we go for the best vendors, with the best products. Even for a haircut, we make sure we do our research and go to only exclusive salons, with the most skilled stylists. But what about when it's time to invest?

242. Investing can be tricky, and the biggest obstacle we face is obligatory investing. We might want to invest with friends or family out of a sense of duty, but let's face it—not everyone we know is a financial whiz. It's important to separate our personal relationships from our financial decisions. Instead of relying on familiar faces, we should prioritise knowledge and experience. You might get your haircut at a friend's salon once, but if you are not satisfied with the services and the prices, would you go there again?

243. Research is key. Bankers have expertise but often lack sincerity. Their main focus is on meeting sales targets and getting promoted to bigger branches in a bigger city. This can make post-sales help a challenge for you as an investor. Similarly, for part-time agents, their job is an additional source of income and they might recommend the wrong product just for an extra commission or a bonus trip abroad.

244. Qualified financial advisors bring years of experience, in-depth knowledge, and a genuine commitment to your financial well-being. They can save you from significant losses. Clear communication, transparency, and a genuine

interest in your financial well-being can turn the stress of managing money into a collaborative and empowering experience.

245. Also, consider your own financial capacity. You wouldn't trust your luxury car with a local mechanic and you wouldn't send a rickshaw to a luxury car mechanic. Similarly, opting for advisors who align with your financial goals is crucial for making well-informed and mutually beneficial investment decisions. Always choose a financial advisor who matches your profile and can understand your financial goals.

246. There is a higher probability that an advisor facing financial challenges might lean towards prioritising immediate revenue. A financially secure advisor on the other hand may place greater value on their reputation and goodwill in the market, rather than solely focusing on additional earnings from your investment. Identify the people who are working for respect over money.

247. Investing with the right people ensures that we're not just safeguarding our money but also setting the stage for long-term financial success. So, let's break free from the pressure of social obligations and invest in our future wisely.

"Your money is your responsibility, blaming others for it is useless."

REAP

Not everyone is fortunate enough to reach this phase in life, but for those who do, it's essential to recognise its value and make the most of it. This phase adds to everything you've already achieved and, while it can happen at any time, it doesn't come often. Unlike the "Run" phase, mistakes made during "Reap" offer little room for correction. It's a fleeting moment, and a single misstep can have lasting consequences.

Success and failure during this phase can be overwhelming. While success is easy to attain, sustaining it requires a resilient mindset. Similarly, only those who can endure failure can stay the course long enough to reach success. The emotional and financial pressures of this time—whether dealing with loans, disputes, or the legacy left by ancestors—can test one's strength. The key is to manage inheritances wisely, maximise what you've been given, and embrace both the rewards and challenges that come with this pivotal phase of life.

Chapter – 39

MOVE ON

In the heart of Guwahati, there was a special record store that had been a part of the town for generations. Started by Nayan's music-loving grandpa in the 1960s, the store was famous, and many local musicians, famous folks, and regular music fans used to visit.

For years, the record store flourished, its shelves adorned with vinyl treasures that echoed the diverse tastes of its patrons. Nayan's family took pride in the legacy that had been passed down to them. The success of the record store brought immense wealth to the family as well. Nayan grew up with luxuries like cars, televisions, and video games that most kids his age had no access to at the time.

However, trouble arrived in the late 1990s with the introduction of the CD. Sales dwindled, and the store, once a bustling haven for music lovers, felt the cold breeze of change. Undeterred, the owners adapted to the times, reluctantly introducing CDs to their inventory.

The shift was slow, and despite their efforts, CD sales struggled to match the heyday of vinyl. Compounding the challenge was the rise of home-burned CDs, as enthusiasts began creating personalised mixes, further denting the store's revenue.

As the 21st century unfolded, digital music became the new trend. The once two-storied store had now been reduced to a quarter its size. Determined and passionate, Nayan, who was now in charge of the store, still held onto it with a sense of duty. Online streaming services ushered in an era where music became accessible with just a click.

Luckily though, Nayan still had a couple of loyal old-school customers that helped keep his business afloat and running.

What do you think Nayan should do moving forward? Will he be able to restore the shop to its former glory?

Points to Ponder:

248. Everyone knows of at least one person who was doing very well financially at some point but lost it all like Nayan's family. This is because they weren't able to adapt to changing times. We believe that what has been working for ages will continue to work for ages to come. Think of how your parents and grandparents lived and your lifestyle now. Our daily routines have drastically changed. Everything from what we eat, to what we wear and even the way we spend our time is completely different, but our earning and investing habits are still the same.

249. If you look at India just post-independence, we had very limited ways of investing money. People had

only three options—putting it in banks, buying gold, or getting real estate. Life insurance was an emerging instrument. Investment decisions back then were based on the limited options that they had. These methods worked fine back then because people had nothing much to spend on either, apart from daily needs and the odd dinner out or a local vacation. But how do old-school ways of investing hold up with our modern lifestyle?

250. We have been influenced by Western ways of spending. We have so many different choices available now, as a result of which our spending habits have changed as well. But if we choose to be stuck in the past when it comes to earning and investing, there is no way we will be able to keep up. Traditional financial instruments worked very well for our parents and grandparents because they led a simpler lifestyle. However, those instruments will not match up with the lifestyle we lead today. Spending and earning are two sides of the same coin. Changing only one side of the coin, without making adjustments to the other is risky.

251. The stock market has been a legitimised and acknowledged way of earning and investing in India for around 50 years now. But lots of folks are still scared to get into it. India is lucky to have a market that's still growing. But if we can't get comfortable with the stock market itself, how do we then even expect to explore and adapt to

even newer instruments that might come our way? Having a vision is key. If we don't change our ways, we might end up becoming obsolete and our wealth will start diminishing, just like Nayan did when he didn't adapt to the digital age.

"Adapt and change with time or fade into history. The choice is yours."

SHADES OF MONEY

In Bilaspur, Mahesh worked as a finance manager at a local firm. His monthly salary was the steady flow that took care of the family's needs. He was known for being prudent with his hard-earned income, managing the household expenses with careful consideration. He saved and invested a portion of his income for his future goals.

He wanted to ensure that he had enough money to pay for his children's education if they ever wished to study abroad in the future. He was saving towards his goal but he was worried about the pace at which he was moving. He had also bought an apartment in the city for his family with the help of a housing loan. After taking care of the loan, and his family's monthly needs, he would be left with very little to save or splurge.

Alongside his job, Mahesh also managed a piece of ancestral property—an old house on the outskirts of Chandipur. It was the house he had grown up in, surrounded by fields and memories. Standing weathered by time, the humble house held the echoes of his childhood. Now that his family had moved into their modern apartment, the old house was left somewhat neglected.

The courtyard, once vibrant with family gatherings, was now overgrown with wildflowers. The creaking wooden floors told tales of generations, but Mahesh didn't have the time or resources to maintain them. The land prices had significantly increased, and he had received several generous offers from builders and other neighbours for the house, making it a tempting sell. Yet, he couldn't bring himself to part with it, held back by sentimental ties to the place he had called home for so many years.

In addition to his monthly salary, Mahesh received a little extra from work—a bonus that felt like a small victory. Grinning, he decided to treat his family to a trip to Dubai and indulge in some luxuries they usually bypassed. The trip itself was something that they would not have been able to afford if not for the bonus. They also went shopping and he bought his son a pair of expensive sneakers. This unexpected financial boost became a special fund for spontaneous joys, making the bonus feel like a bonus indeed.

The same went for any other cash gifts he got from older members of his family. His in-laws gave him and his wife a significant amount of cash as a gift for their fifteenth wedding anniversary. Both Mahesh and his wife instantly spent the money on things they had their eye on for a while. Mahesh gifted his wife a luxury handbag that she had always wanted, while she bought him an expensive watch.

Do you think Mahesh balanced his various streams of income well? Do you think all his streams of income are contributing towards his future goals?

Points to Ponder:

252. We treat different sources of money differently, which can limit our financial choices.

253. Like Mahesh, we treat our hard-earned money with utmost respect, understanding the effort invested to earn it. We recognise its value and spend it carefully. But when it comes to money that has come to us from other sources, we don't treat it with the same respect.

254. Inheritances and ancestral wealth come with their own emotional baggage and are treated as such. Let's say you inherit an FD from your father, there's a sentiment to keep it that way. Because it is *"papa ka paisa"* and he trusted his money in FDs, you prefer to keep it that way. The same goes for gold and real estate. Mahesh couldn't get himself to sell his childhood home despite it not bringing in any real financial profit to him. This emotional connection to how the wealth was accumulated can sometimes lead to decisions that may not be the smartest financially.

255. Approach your inheritance with a sense of gratitude and humility. Recognise it as a privilege, not an entitlement. Maintain a realistic perspective

on it, ensuring it doesn't alter your core values or personality. Only then will you be able to treat it respectfully and optimally.

256. We tend to view bonuses and windfall income as luxury money that is meant to be squandered. The bonus that Mahesh got could have become added income to invest and save; instead, he ended up spending it all immediately on a luxury trip that he could have otherwise never been able to afford.

257. We see any money that is earned from casinos or other means negatively. As a result of this, we don't like holding on to it and spending it all immediately.

258. Any money that is earned by someone else and not you is treated differently and with less value. Like Mahesh and his wife, any cash gifts we receive from elders are seen as personal money that we then use to treat ourselves.

259. Treating all money, regardless of how it comes to us, with the same respect is the first step to making smarter financial decisions. Whether it's money from gifts, businesses, or unexpected wins, pooling them together towards specific goals creates a more unified approach. That way you won't have to wait for other sources of income to spend your money but can plan for your expenses instead.

"Money is money, it knows no bias."

Chapter – 41

BETTING ON TOMORROW

Raghav was a farmer known in his village for growing the sweetest mangoes. Each year, his orchard flourished, and the harvest brought in enough to meet his family's needs and save for the future. This year, however, he had pinned even greater hopes on his crop. The trees were laden with fruit, promising a bumper harvest. With this expectation, Raghav decided it was finally time to repair and renovate his ageing house. Confident that the profits would cover his expenses, he borrowed money from a close friend, planning to repay it once the harvest season paid off.

But nature had other plans. Unusual geographic shifts brought an unexpected storm. The skies darkened, and fierce winds ripped through his orchard. The storm lashed for hours, and when it finally passed, Raghav's heart sank. His once-thriving mango trees lay battered, the fruit scattered and ruined.

When the time came to sell the few mangoes that were still salvageable, Raghav received only 60% of the usual profits, far from the windfall he had counted on. The reality of his situation hit him hard: not only was he unable to make the improvements to his home that he had hoped for, but he also had no means to repay his friend. Raghav found himself in a financial pickle, burdened by commitments he could no longer meet. His dreams of a better life were put on hold, leaving him to face the harsh consequences of his unmet expectations.

Don't you think Raghav shouldn't have begun counting his chickens before they had hatched? Have you been guilty of doing the same?

Points to Ponder:

260. Profit is the financial gain obtained when your revenue exceeds your cost of investment. Notional profit refers to the perceived profit that is yet to be realised. It's a paper gain, calculated based on current valuations or projections, but it hasn't been converted into actual cash or assets.

261. Many people plan their future goals with the assumption that they will inherit property or money. You might inherit some land and real estate that you hope to sell to fulfil your goals. However, this can be misleading. There are so many instances of inheritance disputes that stretch on for years and decades. You cannot base essential financial decisions such as your children's education or your retirement on the expectation of an inheritance.

262. Ancestral wealth should be your plan B. You must reserve them for your aspirations, things you wouldn't normally consider, such as moving into a bigger house. Ancestral wealth is a form of notional profit that most people get carried away with.

263. Credit cards offer a similar illusion of notional wealth. The available credit might make you feel wealthier than you are, leading to spending beyond your means. Before making any purchase, especially large ones, ensure that you have the actual funds to cover it. Make sure the money is actually in your bank account.

264. Spending based on notional profits can lead to overconfidence and poor financial decisions. It's crucial to avoid taking on additional debt based on the appreciation of your assets or potential future earnings. The risk is too high, especially if market conditions change or the expected profit doesn't materialise.

265. When dealing with notional profits or losses, it's important to maintain a balanced perspective. Don't be overly excited about potential gains that haven't been realised. Notional profits can evaporate with market changes or unforeseen events. Likewise, don't be disheartened by notional losses; these are often temporary and can change as market conditions evolve. Always underestimate your profits and overestimate your expenses. This approach ensures that you always have a cushion, reducing the likelihood of financial stress.

"Spend what's in your bank, not in your plans."

REST

The "Rest" phase marks the period of retirement when you can finally let go of the daily grind and enjoy the fruits of your labour. It's a time for relaxation, reflection, and planning on how to pass on your wealth to the next generation. Watching them benefit from what you've built can be one of the greatest joys of this stage. It's also the time to pursue everything you couldn't do earlier—fulfilling passions, hobbies, and personal goals.

However, the ease and enjoyment of the Rest phase are determined by how well you've prepared during the Run and Reap phases. Without proper planning, retirement can become a time of frustration and hardship. Thoughtful financial planning ensures that when it's time to pass on the baton, it becomes a source of strength for the next generation, not a burden. If this transition isn't managed well, it can lead to unnecessary stress and suffering for your successors.

To ensure a fulfilling retirement and a peaceful legacy, prioritise bonding within your family, and ensure that successors receive what they truly deserve. Passing the baton responsibly is crucial for achieving peace of mind, and you don't need to be a multimillionaire to enjoy this phase of life.

Ultimately, how you manage your final responsibilities will define how you are remembered. A well-planned retirement and smooth succession can create a happy ending. If you've fulfilled your earlier stages well, this phase should unfold with ease.

Chapter – 42

LIVING WITH FREEDOM

In the heart of the dense jungle, there lived a lion named Bhanu. In his youth, Bhanu's roar echoed through the trees, commanding respect and fear from all who heard it. His powerful strides shook the earth, and his swift hunts were legendary. The jungle was his kingdom, and he ruled it with strength and dignity.

As the years passed, Bhanu's mane grew silver, and his once unyielding muscles began to soften. It was no longer his responsibility to hunt and bring food for the family, the younger ones took care of it. His steps were no longer as swift, but he still hunted every now and then for his own joy. Though the young lions grew stronger and faster, Bhanu's presence in the jungle was still revered.

One crisp morning, Bhanu ventured into the forest alone, as he had always done. He knew that the days of chasing down prey with ease were behind him, but he had learned something more valuable: patience. Stalking the shadows, he spotted an antelope grazing near the river. With calculated precision, Bhanu moved closer, conserving his energy until the perfect moment. Then, with a sudden burst, he struck, proving that even in his old age, a lion was still a lion.

The jungle watched in awe, as Bhanu dragged his kill back to his den. The younger lions, though stronger, recognised his wisdom and resilience. Bhanu's status as the king of the jungle remained unchallenged, for he had shown that true strength is not just in youth or power, but in the will to endure and the wisdom to adapt.

Although Bhanu is now old, does it take away from his strength and social standing in the jungle? Don't you also want to retire like a lion?

Points to Ponder:

266. We spend our twenties and early thirties focusing on our careers, but when we reach our late thirties and early forties, we slowly start imagining our retirement. The aspirations we have for it. This might include travelling to dream destinations, exploring new hobbies, volunteering for social causes, or furthering your education. If you want to fulfil all this, you need to be financially secure. Just like Bhanu, even in his old age still hunts, the only difference being that he isn't pressured to do so to feed his family. He now hunts, for himself and his leisure. Similarly, retirement doesn't mean that you stop working. It means when your work is no longer a necessity but a choice—if one wishes to engage in it, it does not dictate your hours. Retirement is not just about having a substantial savings account but also having enough to maintain a comfortable lifestyle without the need for ongoing employment.

267. The traditional retirement age is 60-65 years, but this may vary based on your personal circumstances. You can decide to comfortably retire when you have fulfilled all your responsibilities, from buying a home to your children's education and their weddings. For some people, especially if you have had children later in life, this might come later than others. In such cases, if you want to retire on time, you need to plan and make sure you have the funds for all these goals when you decide to retire. Only then will you be able to live comfortably without any worries or you might never be able to retire.

268. Early retirement is an aspirational goal for many, involving stepping away from the workforce before the conventional retirement age. Again, early retirement does not necessarily mean you stop working, it means that work takes a back seat, giving you enough time and money to do everything you had planned. To retire early, one must plan well in advance. This entails saving aggressively, investing wisely, and managing expenditures prudently throughout one's working years. Early retirees often make substantial sacrifices in their earlier years, such as living frugally or investing heavily in growth-oriented assets, to build a financial cushion that allows them to retire sooner than the norm. The allure of early retirement lies in the promise of extra years to pursue passions and live life on one's own terms.

269. In India, the concept of retirement is very challenging and full of fears. You will see so many people, working well beyond their sixties. They are forced to do so, in order to provide for themselves and their families. They find it difficult to envision a future without their regular income.

270. Cultural factors play a significant role. In a society where familial and societal expectations are strong, there's often a prevailing fear of being a financial burden on one's family. This fear compels many to continue working well beyond the traditional retirement age. If we don't have the money to provide for our needs, then we have to earn to not be dependent on our family.

271. Furthermore, the nature of work and retirement planning in India often revolves around real estate and fixed assets rather than liquid financial resources. People rely on these assets for their retirement planning but may find them illiquid or less reliable in providing regular income compared to other financial instruments. If you don't have liquidity, you will be forced to rely on your family and lose respect amidst them. This is why despite having large net worths many older people still lack the freedom to spend their money the way they wish.

272. Many business owners believe that they can always withdraw money from their business during retirement, thinking, "The business is ours."

However, once they reach retirement age, in most cases, their children take over. Just like you were driven towards your business in your younger years, your children too will focus on growing the business. Their priority becomes expansion, which requires funds. Would you, as a parent, be able to ask them to choose your retirement needs over their ambitions? The reality is, that only the money in your bank is truly yours.

"Retirement means the freedom to choose whether to work or not."

Chapter – 43

MONEY WORKS FOR YOU

Dr Ismail Siddique, a paediatrician, embarked on his healthcare journey fifteen years ago in Udupi. Starting small, he charged a humble ₹250 for consultations, seeing a handful of patients each day. It was a slow but satisfying beginning.

Word got around about Dr Siddique's caring approach and medical skill, turning his quiet clinic into a bustling hub for worried parents. The waiting room, once echoing with just a few whispers, now resonated with the laughter and cries of countless children. His dedication to their well-being was genuine, evident in the way he connected with each family.

With growing recognition came a flood of patients, reaching a staggering two hundred a day. The fees, once modest, saw an uptick, reflecting the value placed on Dr Siddique's expertise. However, as his schedule overflowed, the joy he once found in his work started to fade. The very success that brought financial comfort now chained him to a never-ending cycle of appointments.

The irony was hard to ignore—the more patients he saw, the less time he had for himself and his family. Dr Siddique, despite the financial rewards, yearned for a change. The dream of relaxing with family, exploring personal interests, and savouring life's simple pleasures became elusive.

In the midst of a bustling waiting room and a ringing phone, Dr Siddique found himself contemplating a shift. The relentless pursuit of success had left little room for personal moments. His earnings were dependent on his physical presence and the number of patients he saw. He had reached that point where he had begun to question if he wanted to work to earn money or to work to earn time that he could spend on his desires.

What do you think Dr Siddique should do? How can Dr Siddique keep his money growing steadily while taking time off?

Points to Ponder:

273. At some point, you will realise that you've earned enough money and desire to savour life beyond the relentless grind. To ensure a future free from perpetual work, you need to recognise the importance of passive income. Without this realisation, you risk being tethered to work until the end of your days.

274. Passive income, your initial investment sets in motion a self-sustaining system that generates money even when you eat, sleep, and play. There are several forms of passive income, be it rent from real estate properties or interest from safer investment

instruments. But there are also other options that you can explore.

275. Let's say you own a fast-food franchise. The initial investment in itself is a huge amount. You then have to workday in and out and take on running costs and other expenses to generate a steady profit. Now, imagine if you had invested even half that amount in shares of the company instead; your wealth would have multiplied tenfold without lifting a finger. Most people trust companies enough to work with them and depend on them for their livelihood, but not enough to invest in their stocks. We have a huge stake in these companies either way, we might as well invest in their stocks and get an additional source of income.

276. This shift in perspective is crucial. If only Dr Siddique had understood this sooner, he would have moved from being a servant to his income, constantly chasing money, to becoming its master, directing his income to work for him.

"Work to earn time, not just money."

Chapter — 44

THE NET WORTH MIRAGE

In the ancient kingdom of Indrapura, lush with vibrant landscapes and sacred rivers, King Vikramaditya was revered for his wisdom and bravery. The crown jewel of Indrapura's legacy was a powerful sword known as Dharmateja, or 'Sword of Righteousness.' This legendary weapon had been passed down through generations of rulers, known for its ability to cut through any obstacle and its shining aura that could ward off darkness and bring peace.

King Vikramaditya's rule was marked by justice and compassion, as he led his people with a firm yet caring hand. His three sons were trained from a young age in the arts of governance and combat, preparing them for the day they would rule Indrapura. However, the king was afraid that his sons might misuse the sword, and so fiercely protective of the Dharmateja, he kept it locked away in a guarded chamber within the palace. Only the king himself could access the sword. Since he was unable to decide which one of his sons to give access to the sword, he decided that in his absence, all three princes must be present to open the chamber.

One day, King Vikramaditya and his eldest son journeyed to a neighbouring kingdom for peace talks, leaving the two younger princes to govern Indrapura. While they were away, disaster struck. An unexpected attack by invaders from distant lands threatened the kingdom's safety.

The two younger princes rushed to the palace, their hearts pounding with the realisation that they needed the Dharmateja to defend their home. However, upon reaching the chamber, they were met with an impassable door. Without their father and eldest brother, they could not access the sword.

Desperate, they dispatched a messenger on horseback to alert their father of the danger. The princes prayed for the king's swift return, for without the Dharmateja, the kingdom's fate was uncertain.

As the sounds of battle grew closer, the princes anxiously watched the horizon, searching for any sign of their father's return.

Do you think the king and his sons will be able to save their kingdom? What could the king have done to secure his kingdom and future generations?

Points to Ponder:

277. Like King Vikramaditya's sharp and well-maintained sword, money is a powerful tool that can cut through obstacles and create a better life. Learn to treat it as such.

278. Having a powerful sword is beneficial, but keeping it locked away makes it inaccessible, taking away all its power. The same goes for money. Money invested in businesses, especially family businesses, creates the illusion that you are rich. It cannot be easily accessed and spent the way you want to.

279. The princes were aware they had a sword in the family, but when the time came, they had no access to its power. They needed one another to be able to use the sword. Similarly, net worth based on a joint family's collective wealth cannot be accessed until everybody in the family approves of it.

280. Investments in real estate or any other non-liquid asset be it in your name or joint holding with friends and family are also inaccessible because they are difficult to exit.

281. Keeping your money in easily accessible places ensures that it can be used when needed, helping you navigate challenges effectively. It's not just about accumulating wealth; it's about keeping it in a form that can be mobilised when opportunities arise or unforeseen challenges surface. Only the money in your own bank account is your money, your power—the rest is all an illusion.

282. A lot of people don't want to discuss money with their families as they feel guilty for not having done what they had promised or planned to do. However, discussing money openly within a family

is crucial despite the discomfort it may bring. Sharing financial goals fosters a sense of security and prepares everyone for the future. Had the king trusted and trained his sons to access and use the sword, they would have been able to take immediate action when needed.

283. Just as the king's sons in earlier times were trained from a young age to skillfully wield the sword and be worthy of it, you must first make yourself capable and skilled before you start earning money. Social media has promoted the importance of early investments so much that many teenagers and young adults end up using their money on investments instead of bettering themselves. It's not wrong to pursue part-time jobs or start saving early, but not at the cost of your education and skills. It will limit your growth and earning capacity in the future. Prioritise upskilling, especially in your early years. The money you spend on education and self-improvement isn't wasted. The biggest investment you can make is in yourself, and this investment can yield unlimited rewards.

284. A sword cannot be broken into three parts but wealth can be planned so that everyone has access to their own share of net worth. Everyone has different perspectives on life and can lead happy lives only when they have freedom over their own wealth.

"Money holds power only when it can be used."

Chapter – 45

THE EXIT STRATEGY

Under the dim streetlights, two guys lingered outside an apartment building. Vikram, a skinny guy who worked at the store across the street, and Ravi, a big dude up for anything risky, scoped out the Mehta family's flat, 1404. With the Mehtas gone on vacation for a month, it was their chance to score big.

After weeks of watching, they came up with a plan. Vikram knew all about the building's layout and cameras. He even checked out the locks. So, on the chosen night, they sneaked in pretending to deliver groceries. Vikram led the way, dodging the cameras like a pro. They got to the Mehtas' place and busted the lock. Inside, they found cool stuff like electronics and a big TV.

But then they realised they'd messed up. They hadn't figured out how to get out without getting caught. The security guard was lurking, and they were stuck with stolen stuff and no way out.

They panicked, whispering back and forth, trying to come up with a plan. But time was ticking, and they were running out of options. They thought about leaving everything behind and making a run for it, but the temptation of the loot was too strong.

As dawn broke, they were still stuck, realising that no matter how good their plan seemed, things could go sideways real quick. They learned the hard way that sometimes, even the simplest of heists can go wrong.

What lesson do you think this story imparts? Do you think Vikram and Ravi were able to leave with their loot in the end?

Points to Ponder:

285. Ravi's and Vikram's story teaches us that acting without having an exit plan is half the battle lost. It is not only important for us to reach our goals (in the duo's case, breaking into the Mehtas' flat and stealing), but to also get back out safely.

286. It is easy to get caught up in the thrill of growing wealth and why wouldn't it be? We dedicate countless hours to strategizing, investing, and compounding our assets, all with the primary goal of accumulating more money. A lot of people have big net worth but find themselves in difficulty over a few thousand. Growing money is not the end goal in itself; rather, it's a means to an end—the end being the ability to spend that money to achieve our desired lifestyle. Whether it's for retirement, to support our loved ones, or to leave a legacy for future generations, our financial success is truly measured by our ability to enjoy the fruits of our labour.

287. You've diligently saved and invested over the years, building a substantial portfolio that promises financial security for your golden years. But what happens when the time comes to reap the rewards of your efforts? Having assets but not the liquidity to spend at the time of need is like sitting in a metro but not being able to get off at your desired stop because of the crowd. The whole reason you got onto the metro in the first place is to reach that destination and not just to travel. Whether you invest in real estate, equity or your business, you should always have a clear exit plan. A good investment plan with a bad exit plan can be a disaster.

288. When it comes to retirement, a common rule of thumb is The Rule of the Hundred. It suggests that as we age, we should adjust our investment portfolio to reflect our changing risk tolerance and income needs. For example, if you are 60 years old, only 40% of your investments should be in equities, with the remaining 60% in more stable, income-generating assets. This approach ensures we have liquidity during our retirement years.

289. However, if you are not dependent on your retirement corpus and have more money than you will spend in your lifetime, then you can focus on wealth building instead. You can choose to invest more aggressively and build a strong financial legacy for your children.

290. Another thing that people don't expect or plan for is living long. Most people only plan their lives until the age of eighty, but what if you live longer? Our biggest financial fear is passing away early in life, but we can still manage the consequences of it through insurance. The actual fear is living longer than you can afford. If we reach an age where we no longer can generate income, and our savings fall short, we may find ourselves struggling to cover basic living expenses. Even loans are inaccessible to us at that stage in life.

291. People always prefer to live shorter but fulfilled lives, which would have been ideal but our life expectancy is only increasing. We need to have a buffer. You need to keep in mind that you may live an uncharacteristically long life. In case the money does not end up being used, it will simply get passed on to your inheritors. What is more important is that you have it in time of need.

292. An exit plan serves as a roadmap for gracefully transitioning out of investments when the time is right. It provides a structured approach to selling or reallocating assets. It takes into account factors such as market conditions, tax implications, and personal circumstances. As we approach the twilight years of our lives, our investment priorities often shift from wealth accumulation to consumption. An effective exit plan allows us to gradually transition our assets

into more stable and liquid vehicles that you can consume with ease.

"An exit plan ensures you leave with control and security."

Chapter – 46

PERFECT ON PAPER

Naman prided himself on being a modern father, one who treated his son and daughter with equal love and respect. He never discriminated between the two of them, whether it be their education or any other expenditure. When it came to inheritance, he was adamant that his two children, Ashish and Amita, would share everything equally. He decided to leave the factory and the house both in their names. Since he saw them both as equals, he wanted both his children to enjoy his wealth. He had done his job as a parent and was very happy about his decision.

Ashish took over the factory, working long hours to expand the business, while Amita married and moved to another city with her husband. Naman felt satisfied, believing he had done right by both his children. On paper, everything was fair.

But the reality was different. The house, though equally owned, was now occupied by Ashish's family. The business, though half-owned by Amita, was solely run by her brother. She was emotionally attached to the home she grew up in and the business, but that was the extent of it. She could only visit her home as a guest and her connection to the factory was reduced to an annual dividend.

Naman had prided himself on being fair, but in Indian culture, despite parents being modern, daughters often don't ask for their rightful share. Amita, though an equal heir on paper, couldn't access her inheritance because she was hesitant to tell her brother. She was emotionally attached to him and didn't want to inconvenience him by asserting her claim.

Did Amita benefit from her inheritance in all situations? Though the inheritance was equal on paper, who truly enjoyed it?

Points to Ponder:

293. Wealth distribution is a delicate matter, and it's natural for people to consider everyone's opinions before taking any steps. There's a lingering question: "If I do something, will I be seen as a bad person?" This fear of judgement often results in inaction, with many people deciding that their children will simply get whatever they are destined to receive. Many older individuals still struggle with making decisions, particularly when it comes to creating a will or distributing property. They think about it for years but never actually take the necessary steps, leaving their assets in a state of limbo.

294. Naman made a decision, but was it enough? When it comes to planning what we leave behind for our children, making a decision is only one part of your responsibility. Many people believe that simply dividing things equally on paper fulfils their responsibility, however, they often don't do the actual work of ensuring their children will equally benefit from the inheritance. Instead, they comfort themselves with "*Jo hoga dekha jayega*" (Let's see what happens). Naman had decided to leave an equal inheritance to both his children but found it difficult to split things practically. So, he let the decision rest with his children, thinking that he had done his duty. But was that the case? What truly matters is how you see your decision through—planning the implementation is just as crucial as making the choice.

295. It's essential to maintain a healthy balance between attachment to your assets and the willingness to pass them on to your children. Two schools of thought dominate this mindset. One believes that we work hard to ensure our children live comfortable lives, giving them everything during our lifetime. The other clings to wealth, refusing to part with it even when it's no longer needed, believing money should only be passed on after death. However, by that time, children are often older and may no longer benefit as much from the inheritance. Striking a balance between these extremes is key. A true gift

comes without strings attached, and thoughtful timing can make all the difference.

296. The power to distribute inheritance as we see fit is a right granted to us as parents, but are we truly able to exercise it in a way that serves each child's unique needs? While laws may allow for discretion, the emotional and societal pressures of treating all children equally can weigh heavily on decision-making. It's our responsibility to support our children according to their individual circumstances, yet the fear of judgement or guilt may hinder us from providing that tailored support. Do we feel empowered to act on this right? Or are we bound by external expectations and factors?

297. Physical assets, such as property, and business assets are often considered family assets, meaning they are socially regarded as belonging to the entire family. With physical assets, inheritors are by default mentally prepared to receive an equal share. They might see it as unfair and be hurt if they don't receive it. That is how the cultural process around these assets has evolved.

298. There are two solutions to the above problem. You can work in a way in which you can give not just an equal share on paper, but also equal physical possession over those assets. The other way is to create an equivalent amount of liquid assets to give to the child who isn't in physical possession of the properties.

299. The ability to decide what to give and what not to give hinges on having liquid assets. Culturally, you have more privacy and control over these assets, and you can choose to divide them the way you want. These assets offer the flexibility to adjust distributions according to the individual needs of each child. We can only do this effectively if we have liquidity. If we manage it rightfully, our family will remain stronger with no disputes. We must explain to our family why we have divided our assets the way we have to prevent misunderstandings and ensure harmony.

300. Under the pretence of being fair and modern, parents often just do the bare minimum and divide all properties equally between all children. This is also the easiest way for them to be fair without putting too much thought into it. However, when it comes to leaving a legacy, it's important to go beyond merely putting their names on a will.

301. The real question is whether they will actually benefit from the assets. Usually, wealth is enjoyed by the person who has possession of it. If one child moves to another city or country, then only the child with physical access to the asset can benefit from it. They will believe that it is theirs. Even though the inheritance was equally distributed on paper, who is actually enjoying the inheritance? In times of distress, what would Amita have to fall back on? Even if she wanted to sell her share of the

inheritance during bad times, it would have been impractical for her to do so, given that her brother and his family are living in the house and their main source of income is the factory. Selling her portion could disrupt their lives and income, making it difficult for her to access her share without causing tension or financial instability for the rest of the family. Thus, while the inheritance might seem equally divided on paper, practical ownership and benefit can be far more complex.

"Legacy is in the execution, not just the intent."

Chapter – 47

UNTOLD BURDENS

One weekend, twelve-year-old Alika was playing games on her father's laptop when it slipped off the edge of her bed. The screen cracked, and the laptop shut off immediately. Horrified, she tried to turn it back on, but the damage was done. Panicking, she placed the laptop back on her father's desk, too scared to admit what had happened.

Her father, busy with weekend errands, didn't need his laptop until Monday morning when he had an important client meeting scheduled. As he opened it, ready to start the day, he was met with the sight of the cracked screen. Shocked and unprepared, he frantically searched for a solution. With no time to get a repair, he borrowed a colleague's laptop and scrambled to log in to his accounts. The process took longer than expected, delaying the meeting and wasting his client's time.

Afterwards, Alika confessed tearfully to the accident. Her father's face softened, but the frustration was evident. "Alika, if you'd told me sooner, I could've prepared," he sighed. "I would have gone in with a different device and avoided all this chaos."

Alika hung her head, realising how much trouble her silence had caused. "I'm sorry, Dad," she whispered.

He hugged her, saying, "It's alright. Just remember, telling the truth early can save a lot of problems later."

If hiding a broken laptop causes chaos, what about undisclosed debt? Could concealing debt leave your family equally unprepared and overwhelmed?

Points to Ponder:

302. When thinking about your financial legacy, one crucial question arises: Do you want to pass on assets or liabilities? It's not always feasible to repay all your debts within your lifetime, but that doesn't mean you can't plan for it.

303. Just like Alika hid her mistake, leaving her father blindsided during his meeting, many people shy away from disclosing their debts, often due to guilt or shame. However, hiding your liabilities won't make them disappear. In fact, concealing your debt could leave your loved ones in a difficult position after you're gone. Open communication about your financial obligations is essential for proactive planning.

304. Creating a repayment plan is the next step. Consider which assets could be sold to clear outstanding debts. Prioritise debts with high interest rates or those that could significantly burden your heirs. If selling certain assets helps minimise liabilities, it

can provide peace of mind for both you and your family.

305. Open communication with your dependents about your debts is essential. Make sure they understand the nature of your liabilities, your repayment plan, and how these might impact the inheritance they receive. All relevant documents, including loan agreements, insurance policies, and payment records, should be organised and easily accessible. This transparency can help prevent surprises and reduce the emotional and financial stress on your family.

306. Passing on liabilities to your children is not only financially unwise but also puts undue stress on them. This mindset of neglecting debt and leaving it for the next generation is harmful. Instead, approach debt planning with the same level of responsibility and care as asset planning.

307. Just as you work to ensure your heirs receive wealth, you must also strive to prevent them from inheriting your financial burdens. Thoughtful debt planning is an integral part of a sound financial legacy.

"Avoiding today costs more tomorrow."

Chapter – 48

WHEN WISDOM FAILS

From the time he was a young boy, Sukruth harboured a burning ambition to follow in his father's footsteps and become a successful entrepreneur. His father had started a *farsan* shop when he was thirty. The shop had not only provided for their family but also funded Sukruth's happy childhood and education. Inspired by his father's success, Sukruth was determined to carve his own path in the world of business.

Sukruth threw himself into his dream with unwavering determination. He studied business in college, absorbing every bit of knowledge like a sponge, and then pursued an MBA to further refine his skills. He was at the top of his class, and there wasn't any research paper or strategy he hadn't studied. Even after he graduated, he felt like he did not have enough knowledge, so he decided to do an internship. He also enrolled himself in an online course on entrepreneurship which he completed side by side. Finally, at the age of 30, Sukruth felt ready to take the leap and start his venture—a cosy café that would serve as a haven for coffee enthusiasts and pastry lovers alike.

With meticulous planning and boundless enthusiasm, Sukruth poured his heart and soul into his café, envisioning it as the culmination of years of hard work and dedication. However, as the weeks turned into months, Sukruth found himself facing an unexpected reality—the café was struggling to gain traction in the competitive market.

Despite his meticulous planning and tireless efforts, the café struggled to gain traction in the fiercely competitive market.

He had received more knowledge and training than his father at age 30, and despite all his studying and planning, he was unable to achieve what his father had. Disheartened and frustrated by his lack of success, Sukruth turned to his father for guidance. He lamented about his struggles, wondering why his business wasn't taking off as he had hoped, despite all the studying and knowledge he had.

"How did you prepare for your business?" he asked his father.

"I didn't. I just jumped into it. I started my first business when I was twenty. It was a small *there* that sold snacks. I had no other option. It took me years to learn how to run a business. You'll learn it too."

Why did Sukruth's qualifications not translate to business success? Can Sukruth still achieve success despite past setbacks?"

Points to Ponder:

308. While Sukruth spent his twenties gathering knowledge, which is no doubt important, his father had thrown himself into business. He had experienced failures and gained practical, real-life skills. Bookish knowledge can only get you so far, but it is only when you leap that you can truly put your knowledge to use.

309. The truth is, knowledge alone is not enough. It's what we do with that knowledge that truly matters. We can read every book on personal finance, listen to every podcast on investing, and attend every workshop on wealth-building, but if we don't take action, we'll never see the results we desire.

310. We convince ourselves that we need to learn just a little bit more before we're ready to start working towards our goals. We fear making mistakes, so we keep procrastinating, telling ourselves that we'll start tomorrow, next week, or next month. But you're not going to become rich by simply consuming information. Real change only happens when you roll up your sleeves and put that knowledge into action.

311. Start by making notes, jotting down key points, and creating a plan of action. Then, take small, consistent steps towards your goals. It is only when you start investing that you will begin to learn more. Experiment with different strategies, track

your progress and adjust as needed. Remember, it's okay to make mistakes along the way. What's important is that you're taking action and moving forward.

312. If you find yourself feeling overwhelmed or unsure of where to start, don't be afraid to ask for help. Whether it's hiring a financial advisor, or seeking guidance from a mentor, there are plenty of resources available to support you on your journey.

"Knowledge without implementation is wasted."

EPILOGUE

As you move forward, remember that knowledge alone won't get you far. You can read every book on finance, listen to every podcast, and attend every seminar, but none of that will matter if you don't act. We often convince ourselves that we need just a bit more preparation, that we'll start tomorrow or next week. But waiting for the "right time" is just another form of procrastination. The reality is, you're not going to achieve financial success by sitting on knowledge. Action is what moves the needle.

So, start now. Write down your goals, make a plan, and take that first step. It doesn't have to be perfect. As you begin investing, experimenting, and tracking your progress, you'll learn far more than you ever could by reading alone. Mistakes will happen, but they're part of the process. What's important is that you're moving forward, refining your approach, and gaining experience along the way.

If you're feeling uncertain or overwhelmed, don't hesitate to ask for help. Whether from a financial advisor or a mentor, there are plenty of resources to guide you.

One shift in mindset can change everything. Financial independence is about turning knowledge into action and making money a tool that works for you—not something that causes stress. Now is the time to take control.

Best wishes

Garvit